SELECT SERMONS
OF GEORGE WHITEFIELD

SELECT SERMONS
OF GEORGE WHITEFIELD

FORMERLY OF PEMBROKE COLLEGE, OXFORD
AND CHAPLAIN TO THE
COUNTESS OF HUNTINGDON

*

With an account of his life by
J. C. RYLE

and a summary of his doctrine by
R. ELLIOT

THE BANNER OF TRUTH TRUST

THE BANNER OF TRUTH TRUST
3 Murrayfield Road, Edinburgh EH12 6EL
P.O. Box 621, Carlisle, Pennsylvania, 17013, U.S.A.

*

This selection first published 1958
Reprinted 1959
Reprinted 1964
Reprinted 1985
Reprinted 1990
ISBN 0 85151 454 5

*

Reproduced, printed and bound in Great Britain by
BPCC Hazell Books
Aylesbury, Bucks, England
Member of BPCC Ltd.

FOREWORD

It is a privilege to be asked to commend this volume, and to be associated in any way with two such names as George Whitefield and Bishop Ryle.

Nothing has been sadder in the story of the last fifty years in the church, nor more significant, than the way in which George Whitefield has been neglected, and especially as one considers the very considerable attention that has been given to his contemporary, John Wesley. That was certainly not the position two hundred years ago, and it should not be the case now.

Of all the men of the eighteenth century whom God raised up to do that marvellous work called 'the Evangelical Awakening', none was more remarkable than George Whitefield. Of few men can it be said that their preaching was 'apostolic' in character, but it certainly can be said of Whitefield. His whole career from beginning to end was an amazing phenomenon and his Herculean labours both in Great Britain and America can only be explained by the power of the Holy Ghost.

But Whitefield was not only the greatest preacher and orator of the eighteenth century, he was also one of its most saintly characters, if not the saintliest of all. Certainly there was no more humble or lovable man amongst them. What can be more profitable, next to the Bible itself, than to read something of the life of such a man and to read his own words!

This volume provides an excellent introduction. The famous essay by Bishop Ryle is certainly the best short account and evaluation of Whitefield that has ever been done and it is good that it should be thus reprinted. At the same time this volume provides samples of the great preacher's sermons which serve to illustrate the points emphasized by the Bishop. It is a judicious and representative selection.

May God grant that, as we read of the man whom God made so mighty, and the things which he taught and preached, we may be led to long for and to pray for such a revival in our day and generation as God gave in His sovereign grace and mercy two hundred years ago.

February 1958   D. M. LLOYD-JONES
                                   Westminster Chapel
                                   London

CONTENTS

CONTENTS

SERMONS

GEORGE WHITEFIELD
AND HIS MINISTRY

J. C. RYLE

I

Who were the men that revived religion in England a hundred years ago? What were their names, that we may do them honour? Where were they born? How were they educated? What are the leading facts in their lives? What was their special department of labour? To these questions I wish to supply some answers in the present and future chapters.[1]

I pity the man who takes no interest in such inquiries. The instruments that God employs to do His work in the world deserve a close inspection. The man who did not care to look at the rams' horns that blew down Jericho, the hammer and nail that slew Sisera, the lamps and trumpets of Gideon, the sling and stone of David, might fairly be set down as a cold and heartless person. I trust that all who read this volume will like to know something about the English evangelists of the eighteenth century.

The first and foremost whom I will name is the well-known George Whitefield. Though not the first in order, if

[1] These two chapters on Whitefield are taken from Ryle's *Christian Leaders of the Last Century*, published in 1873, part of which has been reprinted by the present publishers as *Five Christian Leaders*.

we look at the date of his birth, I place him first in the order of merit, without any hesitation. Of all the spiritual heroes of a hundred years ago, none saw so soon as Whitefield what the times demanded, and none were so forward in the great work of spiritual aggression. I should think I committed an act of injustice if I placed any name before his.

Whitefield was born at Gloucester in the year 1714. That venerable county-town, which was his birth-place, is connected with more than one name which ought to be dear to every lover of Protestant truth. Tyndal, one of the first and ablest translators of the English Bible, was a Gloucestershire man. Hooper, one of the greatest and best of our English reformers, was Bishop of Gloucester, and was burned at the stake for Christ's truth, within view of his own cathedral, in Queen Mary's reign. In the next century Miles Smith, Bishop of Gloucester, was one of the first to protest against the Romanizing proceedings of Laud, who was then Dean of Gloucester. In fact, he carried his Protestant feeling so far that, when Laud moved the communion-table in the cathedral to the east end, and placed it for the first time 'altar-wise', in 1616, Bishop Smith was so much offended that he refused to enter the walls of the cathedral from that day till his death. Places like Gloucester, we need not doubt, have a rich entailed inheritance of many prayers. The city where Hooper preached and prayed, and where the zealous Miles Smith protested, was the place where the greatest preacher of the gospel England has ever seen was born.

Like many other famous men, Whitefield was of humble origin, and had no rich or noble connections to help him forward in the world. His mother kept the Bell Inn at Gloucester, and appears not to have prospered in business;

at any rate, she never seems to have been able to do anything for Whitefield's advancement in life. The inn itself is still standing, and is reputed to be the birth-place, not only of our greatest English preacher, but also of a well-known English prelate — Henry Philpot, Bishop of Exeter.

Whitefield's early life, according to his own account, was anything but religious; though, like many boys, he had occasional prickings of conscience and spasmodic fits of devout feeling. But habits and general tastes are the only true test of young people's characters. He confesses that he was 'addicted to lying, filthy talking, and foolish jesting', and that he was a 'Sabbath-breaker, a theatre-goer, a card-player, and a romance reader'. All this, he says, went on till he was fifteen years old.

Poor as he was, his residence at Gloucester procured him the advantage of a good education at the Free Grammar School of that city. Here he was a day-scholar until he was fifteen. Nothing is known of his progress there. He can hardly, however, have been quite idle, or else he would not have been ready to enter a University afterwards at the age of eighteen. His letters, moreover, show an acquaintance with Latin, in the shape of frequent quotations, which is seldom acquired, if not picked up at school. The only known fact about his schooldays is this curious one, that even then he was remarkable for his good elocution and memory, and was selected to recite speeches before the Corporation of Gloucester at their annual visitation of the Grammar School.

At the age of fifteen Whitefield appears to have left school, and to have given up Latin and Greek for a season. In all probability, his mother's straitened circumstances made it absolutely necessary for him to do something to assist her in business and to get his own living. He began, therefore, to help her in the daily work of the Bell Inn. 'At length', he says, 'I put on my blue apron, washed cups, cleaned rooms, and, in one word, became a professed common drawer for nigh a year and a half.'

This state of things, however, did not last long. His mother's business at the Bell did not flourish, and she finally retired from it altogether. An old school-fellow revived in his mind the idea of going to Oxford, and he went back to the Grammar School and renewed his studies. Friends were raised up who made interest for him at Pembroke College, Oxford, where the Grammar School of Gloucester held two exhibitions. And at length, after several providential circumstances had smoothed the way, he entered Oxford as a servitor at Pembroke at the age of eighteen.[1]

Whitefield's residence at Oxford was the great turning-point in his life. For two or three years before he went to the University his journal tells us that he had not been without religious convictions. But from the time of his entering Pembroke College these convictions fast ripened into decided Christianity. He diligently attended all means of grace within his reach. He spent his leisure time in visiting the city prison, reading to the prisoners, and trying to do good. He became acquainted with the famous John Wesley and his brother Charles, and a little band of like-minded young men, including the well-known author of *Theron and Aspasio*,

[1] Happening to be at Oxford in June 1865, I went to Pembroke College, and asked whether any one knew the rooms which Whitefield occupied when he was at Oxford. The porter informed me that nothing whatever was known about them. The rooms which the famous Dr Johnson occupied at Pembroke are still pointed out. Johnson left Oxford just before Whitefield went up.

James Hervey. These were the devoted party to whom the name 'Methodists' was first applied, on account of their strict 'method' of living. At one time he seems to have greedily devoured such books as Thomas à Kempis, and Castanuza's *Spiritual Combat*, and to have been in danger of becoming a semi-papist, an ascetic, or a mystic, and of placing the whole of religion in self-denial. He says in his Journal, 'I always chose the worst sort of food. I fasted twice a week. My apparel was mean. I thought it unbecoming a penitent to have his hair powdered. I wore woollen gloves, a patched gown, and dirty shoes; and though I was convinced that the kingdom of God did not consist in meat and drink, yet I resolutely persisted in these voluntary acts of self-denial, because I found in them great promotion of the spiritual life.' Out of all this darkness he was gradually delivered, partly by the advice of one or two experienced Christians, and partly by reading such books as Scougal's *Life of God in the Soul of Man*, Law's *Serious Call*, Baxter's *Call to the Unconverted*, Alleine's *Alarm to Unconverted Sinners*, and Matthew Henry's *Commentary*. 'Above all', he says, 'my mind being now more opened and enlarged, I began to read the Holy Scriptures upon my knees, laying aside all other books, and praying over, if possible, every line and word. This proved meat indeed and drink indeed to my soul. I daily received fresh life, light, and power from above. I got more true knowledge from reading the Book of God in one month than I could ever have acquired from all the writings of men.' Once taught to understand the glorious liberty of Christ's gospel, Whitefield never turned again to asceticism, legalism, mysticism, or strange views of Christian perfection. The experience received by bitter conflict was most valuable to him. The doctrines of free grace, once thoroughly grasped, took deep root in his heart, and became, as it were, bone of his bone and flesh of his flesh. Of all the little band of Oxford methodists, none seem to have got hold so soon of clear views of Christ's gospel as he did, and none kept it so unwaveringly to the end.

At the early age of twenty-two Whitefield was admitted to holy orders by Bishop Benson of Gloucester, on Trinity Sunday, 1736. His ordination was not of his own seeking. The bishop heard of his character from Lady Selwyn and others, sent for him, gave him five guineas to buy books, and offered to ordain him, though only twenty-two years old, whenever he wished. This unexpected offer came to him when he was full of scruples about his own fitness for the ministry. It cut the knot and brought him to the point of decision. 'I began to think', he says, 'that if I held out longer I should fight against God.'

Whitefield's first sermon was preached in the very town where he was born, at the church of St Mary-le-Crypt, Gloucester. His own description of it is the best account that can be given: 'Last Sunday, in the afternoon, I preached my first sermon in the church of St Mary-le-Crypt, where I was baptized, and also first received the sacrament of the Lord's Supper. Curiosity, as you may easily guess, drew a large congregation together upon this occasion. The sight at first a little awed me. But I was comforted with a heartfelt sense of the divine presence, and soon found the unspeakable advantage of having been accustomed to public speaking when a boy at school, and of exhorting the prisoners and poor people at their private houses while at the university. By these means I was kept from being daunted overmuch. As I proceeded I perceived the fire kindled, till at last, though so young and amidst a crowd of those who knew me in my childish days, I was enabled to speak with some degree of gospel authority. Some few mocked, but most seemed for the present struck; and I have since heard that a complaint was made to the bishop that I drove fifteen mad the first sermon! The worthy prelate wished that the madness might not be forgotten before next Sunday.'

Almost immediately after his ordination, Whitefield went to Oxford and took his degree as Bachelor of Arts. He then commenced his regular ministerial life by undertaking temporary duty at the Tower Chapel, London, for two months. While engaged there he preached continually in many London churches; and among others, in the parish churches of Islington, Bishopsgate, St Dunstan's, St Margaret's, Westminster, and Bow, Cheapside. From the very first he obtained a degree of popularity such as no preacher, before or since, has probably ever reached. Whether on week-days or Sundays, wherever he preached, the churches were crowded, and an immense sensation was produced. The plain truth is, that a really eloquent, extempore preacher, preaching the pure gospel with most uncommon gifts of voice and manner, was at that time an entire novelty in London. The congregations were taken by surprise and carried by storm.

From London he removed for two months to Dummer, a little rural parish in Hampshire, near Basingstoke. This was a totally new sphere of action, and he seemed like a man buried alive among poor illiterate people. But he was soon reconciled to it, and thought afterwards that he reaped much profit by conversing with the poor. From Dummer he accepted an invitation, which had been much pressed on him by the Wesleys, to visit the colony of Georgia in North America, and assist in the care of an Orphan House which had been set up near Savannah for the children of colonists.

After preaching for a few months in Gloucestershire, and especially at Bristol and Stonehouse, he sailed for America in the latter part of 1737, and continued there about a year. The affairs of this Orphan House, it may be remarked, occupied much of his attention from this period of his life till he died. Though well-meant, it seems to have been a design of very questionable wisdom, and certainly entailed on Whitefield a world of anxiety and responsibility to the end of his days.

Whitefield returned from Georgia at the latter part of the year 1738, partly to obtain priest's orders, which were conferred on him by his old friend Bishop Benson, and partly on business connected with the Orphan House. He soon, however, discovered that his position was no longer what it was before he sailed for Georgia. The bulk of the clergy were no longer favourable to him, and regarded him with suspicion as an enthusiast and a fanatic. They were especially scandalized by his preaching the doctrine of regeneration or the new birth, as a thing which many baptized persons greatly needed! The number of pulpits to which he had access rapidly diminished. Churchwardens, who had no eyes for drunkenness and impurity, were filled with intense indignation about what they called 'breaches of order'. Bishops who could tolerate Arianism, Socinianism, and Deism, were filled with indignation at a man who declared fully the atonement of Christ and the work of the Holy Ghost, and began to denounce him openly. In short, from this period of his life, Whitefield's field of usefulness within the Church of England narrowed rapidly on every side.

The step which at this juncture gave a turn to the whole current of Whitefield's ministry was his adoption of the system of open-air preaching. Seeing that thousands everywhere would attend no place of worship, spent their Sundays in idleness or sin, and were not to be reached by sermons within walls, he resolved, in the spirit of holy aggression, to go out after them 'into the highways and hedges', on his Master's principle, and 'compel them to come in'. His first attempt to do this was among the colliers at Kingswood near Bristol, in February, 1739. After much prayer he one day went to Hannam Mount, and standing upon a hill began to preach to about a hundred colliers upon Matt 5.1–3. The thing soon became known. The number of hearers rapidly increased, till the congregation amounted to many thousands. His own account of the behaviour of these neglected colliers, who had never been in a church in their lives, is deeply affecting: 'Having', he writes to a friend, 'no righteousness of their own to renounce, they were glad to hear of a Jesus who was a friend to publicans, and came not to call the righteous but sinners to repentance. The first discovery of their being affected was the sight of the white gutters made by their tears, which plentifully fell down their black cheeks as they came out of their coal-pits. Hundreds of them were soon brought under deep conviction, which, as the event proved, happily ended in a sound and thorough conversion. The change was visible to all, though numbers chose to impute it to anything rather than the finger of God. As the scene was quite new, it often occasioned many inward conflicts. Sometimes, when twenty thousand people were before me, I had not in my own apprehension a word to say either to God or them. But I was never totally deserted, and frequently (for to deny it would be lying against God) was so assisted that I knew by happy experience what our Lord meant by saying, "Out of his belly shall flow rivers of living water." The open firmament above me, the prospect of the adjacent fields, with the sight of thousands, some in coaches, some on horseback, and some in the trees, and at times all affected and in tears, was almost too much for, and quite overcame me.'

Two months after this Whitefield began the practice of open-air preaching in London, on April 27, 1739. The circumstances under which this happened were curious. He had gone to Islington to preach for the vicar, his friend Mr Stonehouse. In the midst of the prayer the churchwardens came to him and demanded his licence for preaching in the diocese of London. Whitefield, of course, had not got this licence any more than any clergyman not regularly officiating in the diocese has at this day. The upshot of the matter was, that being forbidden by the churchwardens to preach in the pulpit, he went outside after the communion-service, and preached in the churchyard. 'And', says he, 'God was pleased to assist me in preaching, and so wonderfully to affect the hearers, that I believe we could have gone singing hymns to prison. Let not the adversaries say, I have thrust myself out of their synagogues. No; they have thrust me out.'

From that day forward he became a constant field-preacher, whenever weather and the season of the year made it possible. Two days afterwards, on Sunday, April 29th, he records: 'I preached in Moorfields to an exceeding great multitude. Being weakened by my morning's preaching, I refreshed myself in the afternoon by a little sleep, and at five went and preached at Kennington Common, about two miles from London, when no less than thirty thousand people were supposed to be present.' Henceforth, wherever there were large open spaces round London, wherever there were large bands of idle, godless, Sabbath-breaking people gathered together, in Hackney Fields, Mary-le-bonne Fields, May Fair, Smithfield, Blackheath, Moorfields, and Kennington Common, there went Whitefield and lifted up his voice for Christ.[1] The gospel so proclaimed was listened to and greedily received by hundreds who never dreamed of going to a place of worship. The cause of pure religion was advanced, and souls were plucked from the hand of Satan, like brands from the burning. But it was going much too fast for the Church of those days. The clergy, with a few honourable exceptions, refused entirely to countenance this strange preacher. In the true spirit of the dog in the manger, they neither liked to go after the semi-heathen masses of population themselves, nor liked any one else to do the work for them. The consequence was, that the ministrations of Whitefield in the pulpits of the Church of England from this time almost entirely ceased. He loved the Church in which he had been ordained; he gloried in her Articles; he used her Prayer-book with pleasure. But the Church did not love him, and so lost the use of his services. The plain truth is, that the Church of England of that day was not ready for a man like Whitefield. The Church was too much asleep to understand him, and was vexed at a man who would not keep still and let the devil alone.

The facts of Whitefield's history from this period to the day of his death are almost entirely of one complexion. One year was just like another; and to attempt to follow him would be only going repeatedly over the same ground. From 1739 to the year of his death, 1770, a period of thirty-one

---

[1] The reader will remember that all this happened a hundred years ago, when London was comparatively a small place. Most of the open places where Whitefield preached are now covered with buildings. Kennington Oval and Blackheath alone remain open at this day.

years, his life was one uniform employment. He was eminently a man of one thing, and always about his Master's business. From Sunday mornings to Saturday nights, from the 1st of January to the 31st of December, excepting when laid aside by illness, he was almost incessantly preaching Christ and going about the world entreating men to repent and come to Christ and be saved. There was hardly a considerable town in England, Scotland, or Wales, that he did not visit as an evangelist. When churches were opened to him he gladly preached in churches; when only chapels could be obtained, he cheerfully preached in chapels. When churches and chapels alike were closed, or were too small to contain his hearers, he was ready and willing to preach in the open air. For thirty-one years he laboured in this way, always proclaiming the same glorious gospel, and always, as far as man's eye can judge, with immense effect. In one single Whitsuntide week, after preaching in Moorfields, he received one thousand letters from people under spiritual concern, and admitted to the Lord's table three hundred and fifty persons. In the thirty-four years of his ministry it is reckoned that he preached publicly eighteen thousand times.

His journeyings were prodigious, when the roads and conveyances of his time are considered. He was familiar with 'perils in the wilderness and perils in the seas', if ever man was in modern times. He visited Scotland fourteen times, and was nowhere more acceptable or useful than he was in that Bible-loving country. He crossed the Atlantic seven times, backward and forward, in miserable slow sailing ships, and arrested the attention of thousands in Boston, New York, and Philadelphia. He went over to Ireland twice, and on one occasion was almost murdered by an ignorant Popish mob in Dublin. As to England and Wales, he traversed every county in them, from the Isle of Wight to Berwick-on-Tweed, and from the Land's End to the North Foreland.

His regular ministerial work in London for the winter season, when field-preaching was necessarily suspended, was something prodigious. His weekly engagements at the Tabernacle in Tottenham Court Road, which was built for him when the pulpits of the Established Church were closed, comprised the following work: Every Sunday morning he administered the Lord's Supper to several hundred communicants at half-past six. After this he read prayers, and preached both morning and afternoon. Then he preached again in the evening at half-past five, and concluded by addressing a large society of widows, married people, young men and spinsters, all sitting separately in the area of the Tabernacle, with exhortations suitable to their respective stations. On Monday, Tuesday, Wednesday, and Thursday mornings, he preached regularly at six. On Monday, Tuesday, Wednesday, Thursday, and Saturday evenings, he delivered lectures. This, it will be observed, made thirteen sermons a week! And all this time he was carrying on a large correspondence with people in almost every part of the world.

That any human frame could so long endure the labours that Whitefield went through does indeed seem wonderful. That his life was not cut short by violence, to which he was frequently exposed, is no less wonderful. But he was immortal till his work was done. He died at last very suddenly at Newbury Port, in North America, on Sunday, September 29th, 1770, at the comparatively early age of fifty-six. He was once married to a widow named James, of Abergavenny,

[23]

who died before him. If we may judge from the little mention made of his wife in his letters, his marriage does not seem to have contributed much to his happiness. He left no children, but he left a name far better than that of sons and daughters. Never perhaps was there a man of whom it could be so truly said that he spent and was spent for Christ than George Whitefield.

The circumstances and particulars of this great evangelist's end are so deeply interesting, that I shall make no excuse for dwelling on them. It was an end in striking harmony with the tenor of his life. As he had lived for more than thirty years, so he died, preaching to the very last. He literally almost died in harness. 'Sudden death', he had often said, 'is sudden glory. Whether right or not, I cannot help wishing that I may go off in the same manner. To me it would be worse than death to live to be nursed, and to see friends weeping about me.' He had the desire of his heart granted. He was cut down in a single night by a spasmodic fit of asthma, almost before his friends knew that he was ill.

On the morning of Saturday, September 28th, the day before he died, Whitefield set out on horseback from Portsmouth in New Hampshire, in order to fulfil an engagement to preach at Newbury Port on Sunday. On the way, unfortunately, he was earnestly importuned to preach at a place called Exeter, and though feeling very ill, he had not the heart to refuse. A friend remarked before he preached that he looked more uneasy than usual, and said to him, 'Sir, you are more fit to go to bed than to preach.' To this Whitefield replied: 'True, sir'; and then turning aside, he clasped his hands together, and looking up, said: 'Lord Jesus, I am weary in thy work, but not of thy work. If I have not yet finished my course, let me go and speak for thee once more in the fields, seal thy truth, and come home and die.' He then went and preached to a very great multitude in the fields from the text 2 Cor 13.5, for the space of nearly two hours. It was his last sermon, and a fitting conclusion to his whole career.

An eye-witness has given the following striking account of this closing scene of Whitefield's life: 'He rose from his seat, and stood erect. His appearance alone was a powerful sermon. The thinness of his visage, the paleness of his countenance, the evident struggling of the heavenly spark in a decayed body for utterance, were all deeply interesting; the spirit was willing, but the flesh was dying. In this situation he remained several minutes, unable to speak. He then said: "I will wait for the gracious assistance of God, for He will, I am certain, assist me once more to speak in his name." He then delivered perhaps one of his best sermons. The latter part contained the following passage: "I go; I go to a rest prepared: my sun has given light to many, but now it is about to set – no, to rise to the zenith of immortal glory. I have outlived many on earth, but they cannot outlive me in heaven. Many shall outlive me on earth and live when this body is no more, but there – oh, thought divine! – I shall be in a world where time, age, sickness, and sorrow are unknown. My body fails, but my spirit expands. How willingly would I live for ever to preach Christ. But I die to be with him. How brief – comparatively brief – has been my life compared to the vast labours which I see before me yet to be accomplished. But if I leave now, while so few care about heavenly things, the God of peace will surely visit you".'

After the sermon was over, Whitefield dined with a friend, and then rode on to Newbury Port, though greatly fatigued. On arriving there he supped early, and retired to bed. Tradition says, that as he went up-stairs, with a lighted candle in his hand, he could not resist the inclination to turn round at the head of the stair, and speak to the friends who were assembled to meet him. As he spoke the fire kindled within him, and before he could conclude, the candle which he held in his hand had actually burned down to the socket. He retired to his bedroom, to come out no more alive. A violent fit of spasmodic asthma seized him soon after he got into bed, and before six o'clock the next morning the great preacher was dead. If ever man was ready for his change, Whitefield was that man. When his time came, he had nothing to do but die. Where he died there he was buried, in a vault beneath the pulpit of the church where he had engaged to preach. His sepulchre is shown to this very day; and nothing makes the little town where he died so famous as the fact that it contains the bones of George Whitefield.

Such are the leading facts in the life of the prince of English evangelists of a hundred years ago. His personal character, the real extent of his usefulness, and some account of his style of preaching, are subjects which I must reserve for another chapter.

II

Estimate of good that Whitefield did — Testimonies to his
direct Usefulness — Indirect good that he did — Peculiar
character of his Preaching — Witnesses to his real power as a
Preacher — Simplicity, Directness, Power of Description,
Earnestness, Pathos, Action, Voice, and Fluency, his leading
Excellences — Inner Life, Humility, Love to Christ,
Laboriousness, Self-denial, Disinterestedness, Cheerfulness,
Catholicity — Conclusion

George Whitefield, in my judgment, was so entirely chief
and first among the English Reformers of the last century,
that I make no apology for offering some further informa-
tion about him. The real amount of good he did, the peculiar character of his preaching, the private character of
the man, are all points that deserve consideration. They are
points, I may add, about which there is a vast amount of
misconception.

This misconception perhaps is unavoidable, and ought not
to surprise us. The materials for forming a correct opinion
about such a man as Whitefield are necessarily very scanty.
He wrote no book for the million, of world-wide fame, like
Bunyan's *Pilgrim's Progress*. He headed no crusade against
an apostate Church, with a nation at his back, and princes
on his side, like Martin Luther. He founded no religious
denomination, which pinned its faith on his writings and
carefully embalmed his best acts and words, like John Wesley. There are Lutherans and Wesleyans in the present day,
but there are no Whitefieldites. No! The great evangelist of
last century was a simple, guileless man, who lived for one
thing only, and that was to preach Christ. If he did that, he
cared for nothing else. The records of such a man are large

and full in heaven, I have no doubt. But they are few and scanty upon earth.

We must not forget, beside this, that the many in every age see nothing in a man like Whitefield but fanaticism and enthusiasm. They abhor everything like 'zeal' in religion. They dislike every one who turns the world upside down, and departs from old traditional ways, and will not let the devil alone. Such persons, no doubt, would tell us that the ministry of Whitefield only produced temporary excitement, that his preaching was common-place rant, and that his character had nothing about it to be specially admired. It may be feared that eighteen hundred years ago they would have said much the same of St Paul.

The question, 'What good did Whitefield do?' is one which I answer without the least hesitation. I believe that the *direct good* which he did to immortal souls was enormous. I will go further, – I believe it is incalculable. Credible witnesses in England, Scotland, and America, have placed on record their conviction that he was the means of converting thousands of people. Many, wherever he preached, were not merely pleased, excited, and arrested, but positively turned from sin, and made thorough servants of God. 'Numbering the people', I do not forget, is at all times an objectionable practice. God alone can read hearts and discern the wheat from the tares. Many, no doubt, in days of religious excitement, are set down as converted who are not converted at all. But I wish my readers to understand that my high estimate of Whitefield's usefulness is based on a solid foundation. I ask them to mark well what Whitefield's contemporaries thought of the value of his labours.

Franklin, the well-known American philosopher, was a cold-blooded, calculating man, a Quaker by profession, and not likely to form too high an estimate of any minister's work. Yet even he confessed that 'it was wonderful to see the change soon made by his preaching in the manners of the inhabitants of Philadelphia. From being thoughtless or indifferent about religion, it seemed as if all the world were growing religious.' Franklin himself, it may be remarked, was the leading printer of religious works at Philadelphia; and his readiness to print Whitefield's sermons and journals shows his judgment of the hold that he had on the American mind.

Maclaurin, Willison, and Macculloch, were Scotch ministers whose names are well known north of the Tweed, and the two former of whom deservedly rank high as theological writers. All these have repeatedly testified that Whitefield was made an instrument of doing immense good in Scotland. Willison in particular says, 'that God honoured him with surprising success among sinners of all ranks and persuasions'.

Old Henry Venn, of Huddersfield and Yelling, was a man of strong good sense, as well as of great grace. His opinion was, that 'if the greatness, extent, success, and disinterestedness of a man's labours can give him distinction among the children of Christ, then we are warranted to affirm that scarce any one has equalled Mr Whitefield'. Again he says: 'He was abundantly successful in his vast labours. The seals of his ministry, from first to last, I am persuaded, were more than could be credited could the number be fixed. This is certain, his amazing popularity was only from his usefulness; for he no sooner opened his mouth as a preacher, than God commanded an extraordinary blessing upon his word.'

John Newton was a shrewd man, as well as an eminent minister of the gospel. His testimony is: 'That which finished Mr Whitefield's character as a shining light, and is now his crown of rejoicing, was the singular success which the Lord was pleased to give him in winning souls. It seemed as if he never preached in vain. Perhaps there is hardly a place in all the extensive compass of his labours where some may not yet be found who thankfully acknowledge him as their spiritual father.'

John Wesley did not agree with Whitefield on several theological points of no small importance. But when he preached his funeral sermon, he said: 'Have we read or heard of any person who called so many thousands, so many myriads of sinners to repentance? Above all, have we read or heard of any one who has been the blessed instrument of bringing so many sinners from darkness to light, and from the power of Satan unto God?'

Valuable as these testimonies undoubtedly are, there is one point which they leave totally untouched. That point is the quantity of *indirect good* that Whitefield did. Great as the direct effects of his labours were, I believe firmly that the indirect effects were even greater. His ministry was made a blessing to thousands who never perhaps either saw or heard him.

He was among the first in the eighteenth century who revived attention to the old truths which produced the Protestant Reformation. His constant assertion of the doctrines taught by the Reformers, his repeated references to the Articles and Homilies, and the divinity of the best English theologians, obliged many to think, and roused them to examine their own principles. If the whole truth was known, I believe it would prove that the rise and progress of the Evangelical body in the Church of England received a mighty impulse from George Whitefield.

But this is not the only indirect good that Whitefield did in his day. He was among the first to show the right way to meet the attacks of infidels and sceptics on Christianity. He saw clearly that the most powerful weapon against such men is not cold, metaphysical reasoning and dry critical disquisition, but preaching the whole gospel – living the whole gospel – and spreading the whole gospel. It was not the writings of Leland, and the younger Sherlock, and Waterland, and Leslie, that rolled back the flood of infidelity one half so much as the preaching of Whitefield and his companions. They were the men who were the true champions of Christianity. Infidels are seldom shaken by a mere abstract reasoning. The surest argument against them are gospel truth and gospel life.

Above all, he was the very first Englishman who seems to have thoroughly understood what Dr Chalmers aptly called the *aggressive* system. He was the first to see that Christ's ministers must do the work of fishermen. They must not wait for souls to come to them, but must go after souls, and 'compel them to come in'. He did not sit tamely by his fire side, like a cat in a rainy day, mourning over the wickedness of the land. He went forth to beard the devil in his high places. He attacked sin and wickedness face to face, and gave them no peace. He dived into holes and corners after sinners. He hunted out ignorance and vice wherever they could be found. In short, he set on foot a system of action which, up to his time, had been comparatively unknown in this country, but a system which, once commenced, has never ceased to be employed down to the present day. City missions, town missions, district visiting societies, open-air preachings, home missions, special services, theatre preachings, are all evidences that the value of the 'aggressive system' is now thoroughly recognized by all the Churches. We understand better how to go to work now than we did a hundred years ago. But let us never forget that the first man to commence operations of this kind was George Whitefield, and let us give him the credit he deserves.

The peculiar *character of Whitefield's preaching* is the subject which next demands some consideration. Men naturally wish to know what was the secret of his unparalleled success. The subject is one surrounded with considerable difficulty, and it is no easy matter to form a correct judgment about it. The common idea of many people, that he was a mere common-place ranting Methodist, remarkable for nothing but great fluency, strong doctrine, and a loud voice, will not bear a moment's investigation. Dr Johnson was foolish enough to say, that 'he vociferated and made an impression, but never drew as much attention as a mountebank does; and that he did not draw attention by doing better than others, but by doing what was strange'. But Johnson was anything but infallible when he began to talk about ministers and religion. Such a theory will not hold water. It is contradictory to undeniable facts.

It is a fact that no preacher in England has ever succeeded in arresting the attention of such crowds as Whitefield constantly addressed around London. No preacher has ever been so universally popular in every country that he visited, in England, Scotland and America. No preacher has ever retained his hold on his hearers so entirely as he did for thirty-four years. His popularity never waned. It was as great at the end of his day as it was at the beginning. Wherever he preached, men would leave their workshops and employments to gather round him, and hear like those who heard for eternity. This of itself is a great fact. To command the ear of 'the masses' for a quarter of a century, and to be preaching incessantly the whole time, is an evidence of no common power.

It is another fact that Whitefield's preaching produced a powerful effect on people in every rank of life. He won the admiration of high as well as low, of rich as well as poor, of learned as well as unlearned. If his preaching had been popular with none but the uneducated and the poor, we might have thought it possible that there was little in it but declamation and noise. But, so far from this being the case, he seems to have been acceptable to numbers of the nobility and gentry. The Marquis of Lothian, the Earl of Leven, the Earl of Buchan, Lord Rae, Lord Dartmouth, Lord James A. Gordon, might be named among his warmest admirers, beside Lady Huntingdon and a host of ladies.

It is a fact that eminent critics and literary men, like Lord Bolingbroke and Lord Chesterfield, were frequently his delighted hearers. Even the cold artificial Chesterfield was known to warm under Whitefield's eloquence. Bolingbroke said, 'He is the most extraordinary man in our times. He has the most commanding eloquence I ever heard in any person.' Franklin the philosopher spoke in no measured terms of his preaching powers. Hume the historian declared that it was worth going twenty miles to hear him.

Now, facts like these can never be explained away. They completely upset the theory that Whitefield's preaching was nothing but noise and rant. Bolingbroke, Chesterfield, Hume, and Franklin, were not men to be easily deceived. They were no mean judges of eloquence. They were probably among the best qualified critics of their day. Their unbought and unbiassed opinions appear to me to supply unanswerable proof that there must have been something very extraordinary about Whitefield's preaching. But still, after all, the question remains to be answered, What was the secret of Whitefield's unrivalled popularity and effectiveness?

Let me now point out what appear to have been the distinctive characteristics of Whitefield's preaching.

For one thing, Whitefield preached a *singularly pure gospel*. Few men, perhaps, ever gave their hearers so much wheat and so little chaff. He did not get up to talk about his party, his cause, his interest or his office. He was perpetually telling you about your sins, your heart, Jesus Christ, the Holy Ghost, the absolute need of repentance, faith, and holiness, in the way that the Bible presents these mighty subjects. 'Oh, the righteousness of Jesus Christ!' he would often say; 'I must be excused if I mention it in almost all my sermons.' Preaching of this kind is the preaching that God delights to honour. It must be pre-eminently a *manifestation of truth*.

For another thing, Whitefield's preaching was *singularly lucid and simple*. His hearers, whatever they might think of his doctrine, could never fail to understand what he meant. His style of speaking was easy, plain, and conversational. He seemed to abhor long and involved sentences. He always saw his mark, and went directly at it. He seldom troubled his hearers with abstruse argument and intricate reasoning. Simple Bible statements, apt illustrations, and pertinent anecdotes, were the more common weapons that he used. The consequence was that his hearers always understood him. He never shot above their heads. Here again is one grand element of a preacher's success. He must labour by all means to be understood. It was a wise saying of Archbishop Usher, 'To make easy things seem hard is every man's work; but to make hard things easy is the work of a great preacher'.

For another thing, Whitefield was a singularly *bold and direct preacher*. He never used that indefinite expression 'we', which seems so peculiar to English pulpit oratory, and which only leaves a hearer's mind in a state of misty confusion. He met men face to face, like one who had a message from God to them, 'I have come here to speak to you about your soul'. The result was that many of his hearers used often to think that his sermons were specially meant for themselves. He was not content, as many, with sticking on a meagre tail-piece of application at the end of a long discourse. On the contrary, a constant vein of application ran through all his sermons. 'This is for you, and this is for you.' His hearers were never let alone.

Another striking feature in Whitefield's preaching was *his singular power of description*. The Arabians have a proverb which says, 'He is the best orator who can turn men's ears into eyes'. Whitefield seems to have had a peculiar faculty of doing this. He dramatized his subject so thoroughly that it seemed to move and walk before your eyes. He used to draw such vivid pictures of the things he was handling, that his hearers could believe they actually saw and heard them. 'On one occasion', says one of his biographers, 'Lord Chesterfield was among his hearers. The great preacher, in describing the miserable condition of an unconverted sinner, illustrated the subject by describing a blind beggar. The night was dark, and the road dangerous. The poor mendicant was deserted by his dog near the edge of a precipice, and had nothing to aid him in groping his way but his staff. Whitefield so warmed with his subject, and enforced it with such graphic power, that the whole auditory was kept in breathless silence, as if it saw the movements of the poor old man; and at length, when the beggar was about to take the fatal step which would have hurled him down the precipice to certain destruction, Lord Chesterfield actually made a rush forward to save him, exclaiming aloud, "He is gone! he is gone!" The noble lord had been so entirely carried away by the preacher, that he forgot the whole was a picture.'

Another leading characteristic of Whitefield's preaching was his *tremendous earnestness*. One poor uneducated man said of him, that 'he preached like a lion'. He succeeded in showing people that he at least believed all he was saying, and that his heart, and soul, and mind, and strength, were bent on making them believe it too. His sermons were not like the morning and evening gun at Portsmouth, a kind of formal discharge, fired off as a matter of course, that disturbs nobody. They were all life and fire. There was no getting away from them. Sleep was next to impossible. You must listen whether you liked it or not. There was a holy violence about him which firmly took your attention by storm. You were fairly carried off your legs by his energy before you had time to consider what you would do. This, we may be sure, was one secret of his success. We must convince men that we are in earnest ourselves, if we want to be believed. The difference between one preacher and another, is often not so much in the things said, as in the manner in which they are said.

It is recorded by one of his biographers that an American gentleman once went to hear him, for the first time, in consequence of the report he heard of his preaching powers. The day was rainy, the congregation comparatively thin, and the beginning of the sermon rather heavy. Our American friend began to say to himself, 'This man is no great wonder after all'. He looked round, and saw the congregation as little interested as himself. One old man, in front of the pulpit, had fallen asleep. But all at once Whitefield stopped short. His countenance changed. And then he suddenly broke forth in an altered tone: 'If I had come to speak to you in my own name, you might well rest your elbows on your knees, and your heads on your hands, and sleep; and once in a while look up, and say, What is this babbler talking of? But I have not come to you in my own name. No! I have come to you in the name of the Lord of Hosts' (here he brought down his hand and foot with a force that made the building ring), 'and I must and will be heard'. The congregation started. The old man woke up at once. 'Ay, ay!' cried Whitefield, fixing his eyes on him, 'I have waked you up, have I? I meant to do it. I am not come here to preach to stocks and stones: I have come to you in the name of the Lord God of Hosts, and I must, and will, have an audience.' The hearers were stripped of their apathy at once. Every word of the sermon after this was heard with deep attention, and the American gentleman never forgot it.

One more feature in Whitefield's preaching deserves special notice; and that is, the *immense amount of pathos and feeling* which it always contained. It was no uncommon thing with him to weep profusely in the pulpit. Cornelius Winter, who often accompanied him in his latter journeys, went so far as to say that he hardly ever knew him to get through a sermon without some tears. There seems to have been nothing of affectation in this. He felt intensely for the souls before him, and his feelings found an outlet in tears. Of all the ingredients of his success in preaching, none, I

[37]

suspect, were so powerful as this. It awakened affections and touched secret springs in men, which no amount of reasoning and demonstration could have moved. It smoothed down the prejudices which many had conceived against him. They could not hate the man who wept so much over their souls. 'I came to hear you', said one to him, 'with my pocket full of stones, intending to break your head; but your sermon got the better of me, and broke my heart'. Once become satisfied that a man loves you, and you will listen gladly to anything he has to say.

I will now ask the reader to add to this analysis of Whitefield's preaching, that even by nature he possessed several of the rarest gifts which fit a man to be an orator. His *action* was perfect – so perfect that even Garrick, the famous actor, gave it unqualified praise. His *voice* was as wonderful as his action – so powerful that he could make thirty thousand people hear him at once, and yet so musical and well toned that some said he could raise tears by his pronunciation of the word 'Mesopotamia'. His *manner* in the pulpit was so curiously graceful and fascinating that it was said that no one could hear him for five minutes without forgetting that he squinted. His *fluency* and command of appropriate language were of the highest order, prompting him always to use the right word and to put it in the right place. Add, I repeat, these gifts to the things already mentioned, and then consider whether there is not sufficient in our hands to account for his power and popularity as a preacher.

For my own part, I have no hesitation in saying that I believe no English preacher has ever possessed such a combination of excellent qualifications as Whitefield. Some, no doubt, have surpassed him in some of his gifts; others, perhaps, have equalled him in others. But for a well-balanced combination of some of the finest gifts that a preacher can possess, united with an unrivalled voice, manner, delivery, action, and command of words, Whitefield, I repeat my opinion, stands alone. No Englishman, I believe, dead or alive, has ever equalled him. And I suspect we shall always find that, just in proportion as preachers have approached that curious combination of rare gifts which Whitefield possessed, just in that very proportion have they attained what Clarendon defines true eloquence to be – 'a strange power of making themselves believed'.

The inner life and personal character of this great spiritual hero of the last century are a branch of my subject on which I shall not dwell at any length. In fact, there is no necessity for my doing so. He was a singularly transparent man. There was nothing about him requiring apology or explanation. His faults and good qualities were both clear and plain as noon-day. I shall therefore content myself with simply pointing out the prominent features of his character, so far as they can be gathered from his letters and the accounts of his contemporaries, and then bring my sketch of him to a conclusion.

He was a man of *deep and unfeigned humility*. No one can read the fourteen hundred letters of his, published by Dr Gillies, without observing this. Again and again, in the very zenith of his popularity, we find him speaking of himself and his works in the lowliest terms. 'God be merciful to me a sinner', he writes on September 11, 1753, 'and give me, for his infinite mercy's sake, an humble, thankful, and resigned heart. Truly I am viler than the vilest, and stand amazed at his employing such a wretch as I am.' 'Let none of my friends', he writes on December 27, 1753, 'cry to such a sluggish, lukewarm, unprofitable worm, Spare thyself.

Rather spur me on, I pray you, with an Awake, thou sleeper, and begin to do something for thy God.' Language like this, no doubt, seems foolishness and affectation to the world; but the well-instructed Bible reader will see in it the heart-felt experience of all the brightest saints. It is the language of men like Baxter, and Brainerd, and M'Cheyne. It is the same mind that was in the inspired Apostle Paul. Those that have most light and grace are always the humblest men.

He was a man of burning *love to our Lord Jesus Christ*. That name which is 'above every name' stands out incessantly in all his correspondence. Like fragrant ointment, it gives a savour to all his communications. He seems never weary of saying something about Jesus. 'My Master', as George Herbert said, is never long out of his mind. His love, his atonement, his precious blood, his righteousness, his readiness to receive sinners, his patience and tender dealing with saints, are themes which appear ever fresh before his eyes. In this respect, at least, there is a curious likeness between him and that glorious Scotch divine, Samuel Rutherford.

He was a man of *unwearied diligence and laboriousness* about his Master's business. It would be difficult, perhaps, to name any one in the annals of the Churches who worked so hard for Christ, and so thoroughly spent himself in his service. Henry Venn, in a funeral sermon for him, preached at Bath, bore the following testimony: 'What a sign and wonder was this man of God in the greatness of his labours! One cannot but stand amazed that his mortal frame could, for the space of near thirty years, without interruption, sustain the weight of them; for what so trying to the human frame, in youth especially, as long-continued, frequent, and violent straining of the lungs? Who that knows their structure would think it possible that a person little above the age of manhood could speak in a single week, and that for years – in general forty hours, and in very many weeks sixty – and that to thousands; and after this labour, instead of taking any rest, could be offering up prayers and intercessions, with hymns and spiritual songs, as his manner was, in every house to which he was invited? The truth is, that in point of labour this extraordinary servant of God did as much in a few weeks as most of those who exert themselves are able to do in the space of a year.'

He was to the end a man of *eminent self-denial*. His style of living was most simple. He was remarkable to a proverb for moderation in eating and drinking. All through life he was an early riser. His usual hour for getting up was four o'clock, both in summer and winter; and equally punctual was he in retiring about ten at night. A man of prayerful habits, he frequently spent whole nights in reading and devotion. Cornelius Winter, who often slept in the same room, says that he would sometimes rise during the night for this purpose. He cared little for money, except as a help to the cause of Christ, and refused it, when pressed upon him for his own use, once to the amount of £7,000. He amassed no fortune, and founded no wealthy family. The little money he left behind him at his death arose entirely from the legacies of friends. The Pope's coarse saying about Luther, 'This German beast does not love gold', might have been equally applied to Whitefield.

He was a man of remarkable *disinterestedness and single-ness of eye*. He seemed to live only for two objects – the glory of God and the salvation of souls. Of secondary and covert objects he knew nothing at all. He raised no party of

[41]

followers who took his name. He established no denomina-
tional system, of which his own writings should be cardinal
elements. A favourite expression of his is most characteristic
of the man: 'Let the name of George Whitefield perish, so
long as Christ is exalted.'

He was a man of a singularly *happy and cheerful spirit*.
No one who saw him could ever doubt that he enjoyed his
religion. Tried as he was in many ways throughout his
ministry – slandered by some, despised by others, misrepre-
sented by false brethren, opposed everywhere by the ignorant clergy of his time, worried by incessant controversy
– his elasticity never failed him. He was eminently a rejoicing Christian, whose very demeanour recommended his
Master's service. A venerable lady of New York, after his
death, when speaking of the influences by which the Spirit
won her heart to God, used these remarkable words, – 'Mr
Whitefield was *so cheerful* that it tempted me to become a
Christian'.

Last, but not least, he was a man of extraordinary *charity,
catholicity, and liberality* in his religion. He knew nothing
of that narrow-minded feeling which makes some men
fancy that everything must be barren outside their own
camps, and that their own party has got a complete mono-
poly of truth and heaven. He loved all who loved the Lord
Jesus Christ in sincerity. He measured all by the measure
which the angels use, – 'Did they profess repentance towards God, faith towards our Lord Jesus Christ, and holiness of conversation?' If they did, they were as his brethren.
His soul was with such men, by whatever name they were
called. Minor differences were wood, hay, and stubble to
him. The marks of the Lord Jesus were the only marks he
cared for. . . .

[1]It only remains for me now to point out a few practical lessons.

They are lessons which are strongly impressed on my own mind. Thankful should I be if I could impress them on the minds of others!

1 : In the first place, would we know the right instrumentality for doing good in the present day? Evil is about us and upon us on every side, evil from Romanism, evil from infidelity, evil from tractarianism, evil from neologianism, evil amidst the working classes, evil amidst the educated bodies. What is the true remedy for the disease? What is the weapon to be wielded if we would meet the foe? Can anything be done? Is there no hope?

I answer boldly that the true remedy for all the evils of our day is the same remedy that proved effectual a hundred years ago—the same pure unadulterated doctrine that the men of whom I have been writing used to preach, and the same kind of preachers. I am bold to say that we want nothing new—no new systems, no new school of teaching, no new theology, no new ceremonial, no new gospel. We want nothing but the old truths rightly preached and rightly brought home to consciences, minds, and wills. The evangelical system of theology revived England a hundred years ago, and I have faith to believe that it could revive it again.

There never has been good done in the world excepting by the faithful preaching of evangelical truth. From the days of the apostles down to this time, there have been no victories won, no spiritual successes obtained, except by the doctrines which wrought deliverance a hundred years ago. Where are the conquests of neologianism and tractarianism

---

[1] The rest of this section is taken from the concluding chapter of *Christian Leaders*.

over heathenism, irreligion, immorality? Where are the
nations they have Christianized, the parishes they have
evangelized, the towns they have turned from darkness to
light? You may well ask where? You will get no answer.
The good that has been done in the world, however small,
has always been done by evangelical doctrines; and if men
who are not called 'evangelical' have had successes, they
have had them by using evangelical weapons. They have
ploughed with our heifer, or they would never have had any
harvest to show at all.

I repeat it emphatically, for I believe it sincerely. The first
want of our day is a return to the old, simple, and sharply-
cut doctrines of our fathers in the last century; and the
second want is a generation of like-minded and like-gifted
men to preach them. Give me in any county of England
and Wales a man like Grimshaw or Rowlands or Whitefield,
and there is nothing in the present day which would make
me afraid. I confidently believe that in the face of such men
and such preaching ritualism, neologianism, and infidelity
would be paralysed and wither away.

2: Would we know, in the next place, why the ministers
who profess to follow the evangelical fathers of last century
are so much less successful than they were? The question
is a delicate and interesting one, and ought not to be shelved.
The suspicion naturally crosses some minds, that the doctrines which won victories a hundred years ago are worn
out, and have lost their power. I believe that theory to be
an entire mistake. The answer which I give to the inquiry is
one of a very different kind.

I am obliged then to say plainly, that, in my judgment,
we have among us neither the men nor the doctrines of the
days gone by. We have none who preach with such peculiar

power as Whitefield or Rowlands. We have none who in self-denial, singleness of eye, diligence, holy boldness, and unworldliness, come up to the level of Grimshaw, Walker, Venn, and Fletcher. It is a humbling conclusion; but I have long felt that it is the truth. We lack both the men and the message of the last century. What wonder if we do not see the last century's results. Give us like men and a like message, and I have no fear that the Holy Ghost would grant us like results.

Wherein do evangelical Churchmen fall short of their great predecessors in the last century? Let us look this question fairly in the face. Let us come to particulars. They fall short *in doctrine*. They are neither so full nor so distinct, nor so bold, nor so uncompromising. They are afraid of strong statements. They are too ready to fence, and guard, and qualify all their teaching, as if Christ's gospel was a little baby, and could not be trusted to walk alone. They fall short *as preachers*. They have neither the fervour, nor fire, nor thought, nor illustration, nor directness, nor holy boldness, nor grand simplicity of language which characterized the last century. Above all, they fall short *in life*. They are not men of one thing, separate from the world, unmistakable men of God, ministers of Christ everywhere, indifferent to man's opinion, regardless who is offended, if they only preach truth, always about their Father's business, as Grimshaw and Fletcher used to be. They do not make the world feel that a prophet is among them, and carry about with them their Master's presence, as Moses when he came down from the mount. I write these things with sorrow. I desire to take my full share of blame. But I do believe I am speaking the truth.

It is no use trying to evade the truth on this subject. I

fear that, as a general rule, the evangelical ministry in England has fallen far below the standard of the last century, and that the simple account of the want of success to which so many point is, the low standard both of doctrine and life which prevails. Ease and popularity, and the absence of persecution, are ruinous to some. Political questions eat out the vitality of others. An extravagant and excessive attention to the petty details of parish machinery withers up the ministry of others. An absurd straining after the reputation of being 'intellectual' and original is the curse of others. A desire to seem charitable and liberal, and keep in with everybody, paralyses the ministry of others. The plague is abroad. We want a revival among evangelical ministers. Once let the evangelical ministry of England return to the ways of the last century, and I firmly believe we should have as much success as before. We are where we are, because we have come short of our fathers.

3: Last of all comes the all-important question, What ought we to do? I answer confidently, There are three things which we shall do well to remember, if we wish our work to prosper.

First, let us resolve to cast in our lot boldly on the side of what I must call 'evangelical' religion in England. Let us not be moved by the sneers and contempt which are poured on it in some quarters. Let us cleave to it, hold it fast, and never let it go. Let us beware of the plausible charity which says, 'All earnest men hold the truth. No earnest man can err.' Let us beware of the idolatry of intellect, which says, 'A man cannot make mistakes in doctrine if he is a clever man'. Of both these dangers let us beware. Let us lay hold firmly on evangelical religion as the truth of God, and never be ashamed to confess it. Let us stand by it, and it will stand by us in the hour of sickness and on the bed of death, in the swellings of Jordan, and in the day of judgment.

Next, let us resolve to work heartily for evangelical truth, each in his own place. There is always work for every one before his own door. Let us never stand still because we are in a minority. What though we stand alone in a house of business, alone in the banking-house, alone in a regiment, alone in a ship, alone in a family! What of it? Let us think of the little company who shook England one hundred years ago, and work on. It is truth, not numbers, which shall always in the end prevail. The three hundred at Thermopylæ were better than the million of Persians. A small minority of evangelical Christians with the gospel in their hearts are stronger than a host of servants of the Pope, the devil, and the world.

And let us pray, last of all, as well as work. Let us pray night and day that God would revive his work in England, and raise up many more instruments to do his will. Let us pray with the abiding thought that God's arm is not shortened, that what he has done he can do again, and that the same God who wrought so mightily for England one hundred years ago can do greater things still. Let us ask Him who holds the stars in his right hand to revive his work among our ministers, and to raise up men for our times. He can do it. He is willing to do it. He waits to be entreated. Then let all who pray cry night and day to the Lord of the harvest, 'Lord, send forth more labourers into thy harvest'.

A SUMMARY OF
GOSPEL DOCTRINE

R. ELLIOT

A SUMMARY OF
GOSPEL DOCTRINE
TAUGHT BY
MR WHITEFIELD

recorded in a funeral sermon
on his death by

R. ELLIOT, BA[1]

Mr Whitefield was no partisan in religion. His spirit was not narrow and contracted, but he cordially embraced all the true followers of Christ, of every opinion, name and nation, however in circumstantials, modes, and external forms of worship they might differ from him: yet he was zealous, steady, and unshaken in the great and fundamental truths of the Gospel. There are some, I hear, who would insinuate that, towards the close of his life, he began to change his sentiments on some of those important points: but I can hardly think that any one but those of the contrary opinions whom he opposed, and who wished to have it so, will credit the report. What were his real sentiments must be collected from his printed works, especially as he never to the last, either from the pulpit or the press, retracted or disavowed any of them: consequently he died in those principles which thirty years ago he preached and defended.

And now, my friends, let me point out to you those great truths of the Gospel which Mr Whitefield in his life-time preached and insisted on. The doctrines that he held and

---

[1] Elliot was converted under Whitefield's early ministry. He later became a prominent minister, and an intimate connexion between him and Whitefield was formed.

taught are, I conceive, the chief thing which we are to regard and hold fast; not that any doctrine, without a suitable and holy practice, will profit to the salvation of them that hold it, for the faith of God's elect is a most holy faith, and the truths of the Gospel are ever according to godliness; but as it is plain that the general practice of all men is according to the principles which they hold, so it is certain that a man cannot be sound at heart nor holy in life that doth not hold a sound and wholesome doctrine. An Antinomian in principle is the same in his hope and conversation; he expects to be saved at last, though he continues to live in sin: And an Arminian, or one who is a legal free-willer in his principles, expects to be accepted of God, and saved at last; not for the sake of Christ, and of God's free sovereign grace only, but for what he himself hath done either in part or in whole; and to this all his willing, running, and working tends.

But Mr Whitefield kept clear of both these equally dangerous extremes. The great doctrines which he taught and insisted on were: (1) Original sin; (2) The new birth; (3) Justification by faith in Christ; (4) The final perseverance of the saints; (5) Eternal and unconditional election. And if I am not mistaken, he held and taught the first three in a very different manner from some persons who would be thought to hold and teach them too. But we must understand and mean the same things by the same expressions before we can be said to hold the same doctrines.

1: He taught the Scripture doctrine of original sin, which consists in these two things: First, Adam's personal offence imputed; and, second, the entire depravity of his fallen nature, imparted to all his seed. By the former we are held faulty and stand guilty in our persons before God:

and by the latter our natures are corrupted, prone to sin, and naturally inclined to all evil: and thus it is written: 'By the offence of one, judgment came upon all men to condemnation.' And again it is written: 'Every imagination of the thought of man's heart is only evil continually.' Hence we are all by nature sinners and children of wrath. The Church of England also bears her testimony to the truth of this alarming and awful doctrine in the ninth article of her faith, in which she asserts that 'Original sin is the fault and corruption of the nature of every man that naturally is engendered of the offspring of Adam, whereby man is very far gone from original righteousness, and is of his own nature inclined to evil', etc. The fault is from Adam's offence imputed; our corruption, and propensity to evil, is from the depravity of his sinful nature communicated and imparted to us.

2: Hence, the Scripture doctrine of regeneration appears suitable to the deplorable circumstances, and expedient for the relief of fallen man. The new birth, our departed friend diligently taught and insisted on as absolutely necessary to salvation. Of this doctrine, our Lord, in St John's Gospel, Ch. 3, speaks largely, and testifies the necessity of it: he there assures us, that except a man be born again, of water and of the Spirit, he cannot enter, nor even see, the kingdom of God. The understanding of men by nature is darkness, the will obstinate and rebellious, the heart hard and obdurate, the affections wedded and enslaved to lusts and pleasures, and the whole carnal mind is enmity against God. Hence the necessity of such an entire change as may with propriety be called 'A new creation'. Every man whilst in his natural state, though ever so refined by education and decent in his morals, is at enmity with God and is continually rebelling against him: therefore he must be changed and renewed in the spirit of his mind, else he can have no true love for God and for the Lord Jesus Christ.

Mr Whitefield taught concerning the new birth, that man by nature has no power or will at all to come to God and save himself. It is indeed manifestly absurd, and it implies a contradiction, to suppose that a man can be the cause of his own existence; or that he hath power to change his present fallen condition, when it implies a change of his heart and will, and comprehends in it a new creation. Therefore man has no power or will at all to effect his own conversion, it being the entire work of God's Spirit: Mr Whitefield also very consistently maintained that the grace of God in the conversion of a sinner is irresistible; and indeed he who denies it cannot truly believe that man is entirely fallen, or preach in the manner that he did the doctrine of the new birth, for that which is effected by the will of man in any sense, and not by the alone sovereign irresistible grace of God, is not the change that Mr Whitefield called, and the Scripture terms, the new birth.

3: The doctrine of justification by faith in Christ, he diligently and constantly taught: but he held faith not as our justifying righteousness, but only as the instrument of our justification, which some that profess to teach the same doctrine absolutely deny: we are justified, said Mr Whitefield, three ways, viz.: (1) Meritoriously by the blood of Christ; (2) Instrumentally by the faith of Christ; and (3) Declaratively by our good works. And when speaking of being justified by faith, he would always direct the sinner to Christ's blood and righteousness as the only proper procuring cause of his justification. He did not, as some others, put man's free will in the room of God's free grace, and our act of believing in the place and stead of Christ's obedience. 'For the sake', saith he, 'of Christ's righteousness alone, and not for any thing wrought in us, doth God look favourably upon us; we must therefore look for a righteousness without us, even the righteousness of our Lord Jesus Christ. Whosoever teacheth any other doctrine doth not preach the truth as it is in Jesus.' Thus he maintained (*a*) that the perfect personal surety-righteousness of Christ is of God imputed to believers for their justification; (*b*) that the Scripture doctrine of original sin and our fall in Adam, whose personal disobedience is imputed to us, implies the necessity of it: and (*c*) that God intended thus to justify his people by imputing to them his Son's righteousness, as the apostle testifies, Rom 5. To deny this, what is it but in effect to deny that Adam's offence was imputed to us? Here observe, that the personal obedience of Christ, which is reckoned to all believers, is not inherent in them, nor can it be properly imparted to any believer, but is imputed only. Thus we must carefully distinguish between that righteousness whereby a believer is justified, and that holiness whereby he is sanctified: that whereby he is justified (I speak of justification before God) is the obedience of Christ to the whole law in the sinner's stead, which obedience he finished upon the cross; but that holiness whereby we are sanctified is the purification and renewal of our natures by the Spirit of Christ. The former is the work of Christ without us, the latter is the work of his Spirit within us: THAT is imputed. and THIS is imparted: for as a sinner cannot be sanctified by an imputed holiness, so neither can he be justified by an imparted righteousness. Thus as the work of the Holy Spirit within us, regenerating and renewing our souls, cleanses and relieves us from the defilement and corruption of our natures, communicated to us, and inherent in us; so the finished work of Christ's obedience without us, but imputed to us, doth relieve and justify us from the guilt and condemnation of Adam's sin imputed to us, and from all our own personal transgressions: for as by the disobedience of one, many were made sinners, so by the obedience of one shall many be made righteous, Rom 5.19. And this is far more evident yet, in that our sins were laid upon Christ, and he as our surety took them upon him, and was made under the law for our sakes; consequently his doing and suffering must be reckoned and placed to our account, that we may receive the blessing and benefit thereby obtained, and purchased for us: and so it is written, God hath made him to be sin for us, who knew no sin, that we might be made the righteousness of God in him, 2 Cor 5.21. Thus is Christ the end of the law for righteousness to every one that believeth, Rom 10.4.

4: He taught and maintained the final perseverance of the saints; not indeed by the power of their own free will, nor by virtue of their own faithfulness, but by the power and faithfulness of God; for whom he justified, them he also glorified, Rom 8.30. He hath also engaged to keep them in a way of holiness, and so to secure their standing in Christ by faith: wherefore he saith, 'faithful is he that calleth you, who also will do it', 1 Thess 5.24, and thus Mr Whitefield expressly taught. Never, saith he, did God justify a man whom he did not sanctify, nor sanctify one whom he did not completely redeem and glorify. Nor did he stop here, for, enquiring at the mouth of the Lord, that is of the Holy Scriptures, why and whence it is that these great and inestimable gifts and blessings are given to miserable sinners of the human race, he understood and believed that Christ, and together with him all things, were freely given to them of God's mere good pleasure, who worketh all things after the counsel of his own will, Eph 1.5.

5: Therefore, in the next place, he held, taught and defended the Scripture doctrine of God's eternal unconditional election. Thus, in the letter before referred to,[1] he speaks of and contends for it in the most convincing, instructing, and edifying manner. Some men cannot bear this doctrine, and others consider it as a point of no great moment: but did Mr Whitefield thus consider it, or treat it as a circumstantial only? No, certainly! He held it possible indeed that a man might be in a state of grace, and yet not hold this doctrine, but he counted it a bad sign in those that deny it, for he speaks of it as a doctrine whereby God is eminently glorified and his people greatly edified and comforted, and he plainly declares that they who do not believe it cannot hold aright the Scripture doctrine of original sin: and for my own part, I verily believe so too: And when any man opposed it violently, he would speak doubtfully of that person though in other respects he might highly esteem and honour him.

In the letter above referred to, in which he maintains and defends the doctrine of election against his opposer, he considers and answers the most plausible objections which are commonly made against it. First, they say that this doctrine makes people doubt of their state, and throws them into despairing fears, etc. He answers, 'So does the doctrine of regeneration, but is not this doubting, a good means to make their calling and election sure? This is one reason among

[1] This letter which Elliot first speaks of in the preface to his sermon, is Whitefield's reply to John Wesley on the subject of free-grace. The letter is dated December 24, 1740, and is reprinted in *Whitefield's Journals* by the present publishers.

many others why I admire the doctrine of election, and am convinced that it should have a place in a Gospel ministry. It has a natural tendency to rouse the soul out of its carnal security, and therefore many carnal men cry out against it: whereas universal redemption is a notion sadly adapted to keep the soul in its lethargic sleepy condition, and therefore so many natural men admire and applaud it.' His heart indeed seems to be enlarged upon this subject. There is, I suppose, no one point of doctrine that he has treated of so particularly and so fully as this. Many objections are herein considered and refuted, and I hope that some of his friends will have grace and courage enough to republish it for the benefit of his surviving friends and of Christians in general, for it is a concise, clear and admirable defence of that important doctrine.

He maintains it to be a most comfortable and establishing doctrine to true believers, and that the contrary opinion is hurtful and distressing; for on p. 18, he says 'Many have an assurance that they are in Christ to-day, but take no thought for, or are not assured that they shall be in him, tomorrow, nay to all eternity. This is rather their imperfection and unhappiness than their privilege. I pray God to bring all such to a sense of his eternal love, that they may no longer build upon their own faithfulness, but on the unchangeableness of that God whose gifts and callings are without repentance: for that (viz., universal redemption), I am sure, has a natural tendency to keep the soul in darkness for ever; because the creature thereby is taught, that his being kept in a state of salvation is owing to his own free-will. And what a sandy foundation is that for a poor creature to build his hopes of perseverance upon! Every relapse into sin, every surprise by temptation, must throw him into doubts and fears', etc.

If it be again objected that the doctrine of election and the sovereignty of God in calling whom he will, has a tendency to encourage sloth and licentiousness, he (Mr Whitefield) disavows and abhors the thought, and boldly asserts and proves the contrary, both from his own experience, and also from that of his Christian friends.

'It is the doctrine of election (says he) that mostly presses me to abound in good works. I am made willing to suffer all things for the elect's sake. This makes me preach with comfort, because I know salvation doth not depend on man's free-will, but the Lord makes them willing in the day of his power, and can make use of me to bring some of his elect home, when and where he pleases.' If I am constrained by the love of God to love him again, then by how much the more I apprehend and believe the freeness, greatness and unchangeableness of his love towards me, by so much the more am I made willing and enlarged in my heart to honour, serve and glorify him. The contrary doctrine hath a tendency to make a soul settle upon his natural bottom of free-will and self-righteousness. Is it again objected that it destroys the use of means, and makes preaching vain? He answers, 'Hath not God, who appointed salvation for a certain number, appointed also the preaching of the Word as a means to bring them to it?' etc. Is it again further objected, that it tends to destroy holiness? He answers, 'Whoever preached any other election than what the apostle preached, when he said, "Chosen to salvation through sanctification of the Spirit"? Nay, is not holiness made a mark of our election by all that preach it? and how then can the doctrine of election destroy holiness?' And addressing himself to the opposite party, he says, 'Those who settle in the universal scheme, though they might begin in the Spirit, yet (whatever they may say to the contrary) are ending in the flesh; and building up a righteousness founded on their own free-will'. This, if true, and I think it agreeable to Scripture, is an awful passage to obstinate universalists. And a little after, he saith, p. 19: 'You plainly make salvation depend not on God's free grace, but on man's free-will'; or as he speaks in another place, 'You cannot make this assertion good, that Christ died for them that perish, without holding that all the damned souls shall hereafter be brought out of hell: for how can all be universally redeemed, if all are not universally saved?' And it seems to be from one or other of these reasons, that all Arians, Socinians, and Antinomians, as well as Arminians, hold universal redemption.

To their grand objection to this doctrine, viz. that we thereby charge God with injustice (which St Paul supposes, and rejects with abhorrence) by unchangeably dooming to everlasting burnings thousands and millions of men, without any preceding offence and fault of theirs: he thus replies, 'But who ever asserted that thousands and millions of men, without any preceding offence or fault of theirs, were unchangeably doomed to everlasting burnings? Do not they who believe God's dooming men to everlasting burnings, also believe that God looked upon them as men fallen in Adam? And that the decree which ordained the punishment, first regarded the crime by which it was deserved? How then are they doomed without any preceding fault? Surely you (Mr Wesley) will own God's justice in imputing Adam's sin to his posterity; and also, that after Adam fell, and his posterity in him, God might justly have passed them ALL by, without sending his own Son to be a Saviour for any one.' 'Unless you heartily agree to both these points, you do not believe original sin aright. If you do own them, then you must acknowledge the doctrine of election and reprobation to be highly just and reasonable. For if God might justly impute Adam's sin to all, and afterwards have passed by all, then he might justly pass by SOME. Turn on the right hand, or on the left, you are reduced to an inextricable dilemma. And, if you would be confident, you must either give up the doctrine of the imputation of Adam's sin, or receive the amiable doctrine of election, with a holy and righteous reprobation as its consequent. For whether you can believe it or not, the Word of God abides faithful. "The election hath obtained it, and the rest were blinded".' Thus he taught, and thus he wrote.

This Letter was printed thirty years ago, and in it you may see much more to the same purpose on this subject: but I fear some, who call themselves Mr Whitefield's friends and followers, are strangers both to him and his doctrine. Many perhaps might follow him from carnal motives, but unless they hold his principles, they cannot with propriety be called his followers, for the sake of those truths which he held and taught.

He considered the doctrine of election as a branch of that faith spoken of by Jude, for which we are bid to contend earnestly: and therefore in defence of it, he opposes his most dear and intimate friend, with all zeal and faithfulness; and I have heard him say, that the doctrine of universal redemption is at the bottom of their errors, i.e. of those who deny justification by Christ's imputed righteousness, the final perseverance of the saints, and hold in an absolute sense, sinless perfection: but the doctrine of election, and that only, makes salvation to be by grace alone.

I proceed, lastly, to make an application by way of improvement.

And First. If we have been hearers of Mr Whitefield, and loved him for Christ's sake and the Gospel, we should strive to make it manifest by continuing to hold fast those precious truths which we have heard from him, not only whilst he was present with us, but also, now he is taken from us; and that by contending earnestly for them against all opposers as he himself did: not because they were his doctrines, but the doctrines of God and of Christ, of all the holy prophets and apostles, as the Scriptures abundantly testify. He condemned the unscriptural notion of universal redemption, because it 'opposes the truth as it is in Jesus, casts the highest reproach upon the dignity of the Son of God, and the merit of his blood, and leads men to depend not on God's free grace, but on their own free will'; and is therefore a doctrine dishonourable to God, and destructive to souls.

If universal redemption, taken in a literal sense, be admitted, the equally unscriptural notions of universal salvation, or of justification by works, and salvation by man's free-will, together with that of the possibility of falling away from the state of grace, totally and finally, must unavoidably follow: but the Scripture asserts and testifies, that salvation is wholly of God, and not of the will of man; by grace, and not of works lest any man should boast. Remember therefore how the Gospel of Christ hath been preached unto you, and received by you. Did your dear minister and faithful servant of Christ preach the Gospel unto you, as one that must give an account? So must you also give an account of your hearing. Beware that you do not let these doctrines of God's grace slip from you, but keep them in memory and contend for them; and let none persuade you to think lightly and meanly of them; for how shall we escape if we neglect so great salvation? Take heed also, my brethren, how you hear, for many seem to call that grace, and faith and the new birth, which are not so in truth. This is the artful design of those whose principles are corrupt at bottom; thus they make use of the same words and expressions, but apply them to their own notions and opinions; hence by the same words and phrases they mean very differently from what the apostles meant and Mr Whitefield taught: whoever according to him received not the doctrine of election, 'doth not believe original sin aright': wherefore he saith again, 'You must either give up the doctrine of the imputation of Adam's sin, or receive the amiable doctrine of election, with a holy and righteous reprobation as its consequent'. Were it now possible for him to address his dear hearers as he was wont to do, think you not that he would loudly declare, and testify that the new birth is the soul's regeneration, by the sovereign irresistible grace of God's Spirit, without the concurrence and will of man? that justification through faith, is by the righteousness of Christ without us, but imputed to us? and that whom he justifies he will assuredly sanctify and glorify? See then that ye continue in the faith grounded and settled, lest by any means you should be moved away from the hope of the Gospel, for it is a good thing to have the heart established with grace. Grace in Scripture is set in opposition to man's worthiness, faith to works, the righteousness of Christ to man's righteousness, the power of God to man's ability, and the security of the salvation of God's chosen believing people is entirely laid and rests on Christ's sufficiency, and God's immutability, faithfulness and truth.

2: Mr Whitefield did not hold, nor teach these Gospel doctrines but in a way of holiness, and according to godliness. He was no libertine, no Antinomian in principle or practice. He maintained also, and we believe, that these doctrines of grace do not only more freely and abundantly promote holiness than those of the contrary persuasion, but that these doctrines alone can effectually influence believers to practical religion, in a right and holy manner. I beseech you therefore, brethren, to evidence your election by obedience to the Gospel, your faith by good works, your abiding in Christ by following after charity, peace with all men, and holiness; for it is an undoubted truth, that every doctrine that comes from God leads to God; and that which doth not tend to promote holiness is not of God. That doctrine, whose tendency is not to destroy sin, can never be to the praise of God's glorious grace; for the grace of God, which bringeth salvation to men, teacheth us, that denying all ungodliness and worldly lusts, we should live righteously, soberly and godly in this present world. Put on therefore as the elect of God, holy and beloved, bowels of mercies, humbleness of mind, meekness, long-suffering, forbearing and forgiving one another, as God for Christ's sake hath forgiven you: and thus make it manifest by a holy life and conversation, that this is the true grace of God that ye have received, and wherein ye stand. So shall you shame your adversaries of the contrary side who falsely accuse your good conversation in Christ. Oh! that none of you may rest in a lukewarm, formal profession, having a name to live whilst you are dead. Interrogate then, and thoroughly examine into the state and circumstances of your own souls. Let not the world, i.e. the lusts and love of it, be admitted to a share of your hearts with Christ, for he saith, 'Whoever he be of you, that forsaketh not all that he hath, cannot be my disciple'. This seems to many to be a hard saying at which they are offended, and by departing from him, with the multitude, or forsaking his cause and servants, with

Demas, they manifest themselves not to have been his disciples indeed; for they that are truly such continue in the faith, and he that endureth to the end, the same shall be saved.

3: Let us boldly maintain, and earnestly contend for the faith of God's elect, with becoming zeal, and in the spirit of meekness. Our adversaries are ever watching for our halting. All their policy and power is constantly engaged to do us mischief. They will do what in them lies, by corrupting the Scriptures, to darken the truths of God, and wrest them out of our hands; and would, if it were possible, deceive the very elect: we must therefore wrestle, and fight, and pray to be kept in the faith, lest by admitting their errors, we should fall from our own steadfastness. 'I came not', saith Christ, 'to send peace on the earth but a sword.' We must not then tamely yield up, or quietly suffer ourselves to be robbed of the saving doctrines of grace, but obstinately fight and per-severingly contend for them. Some disaffected or sickly minds will not only themselves avoid, but censure those who warmly oppose errors and are strenuous in defence of the truth; but this, to say no worse of it, is their weakness: for had Mr Whitefield thought so, he never would have preached or written against the errors of his most intimate friend, in the manner that he hath done. If the apostle Paul had thought and done so, there would have been no epistles to the Galatians, Corinthians, Philippians, or Colossians. When errors are springing up, there must be a bold stand made against them, let who will be the propagators and maintainers of them.

Beware they do not beguile you with enticing words, by saying these are points of no great moment, mere opinions, circumstantials only, wherein good men in all ages have thought differently; for it is quite otherwise when the difference respects the doctrine of salvation by grace; for in this matter, a little leaven leaveneth the whole lump. I beseech you therefore, brethren, mark them which cause divisions and offences contrary to the doctrine which you have received, and avoid them, for they that are such serve not our Lord Jesus Christ, but their own bellies, and by flattering words, and fair speeches, deceive the hearts of the simple (Rom 16.17–18). The greatest and most dangerous errors, whereby the church of God hath been troubled and hurt in all ages, have arisen not from avowed enemies without, but from professed friends within: in the Apostles' days there were Antinomians and legal free-willers, both which are by him condemned, and the churches warned of them; but especially the latter, because they appeared in the garb of professed friendship, holiness and love and were themselves in appearance as ministers of righteousness; and these are the persons who seem to have charged the Apostle with walking after the flesh (2 Cor 10.2). Beware then, that through credulity and weakness you do not receive their erroneous opinions.

4: Let us be prepared, and ready to follow our departed friend, for we know not the day nor the hour when our Lord will come; it seems indeed as if the Lord is about to visit us in judgment, both as a nation and a church: as a nation for the exceeding profaneness, filthiness, infidelity, luxury and oppression, that appears everywhere to prevail amongst us. We cannot indeed certainly tell whether his judgments will be speedily poured out upon us or not, but we have great reason to fear it; war and the pestilence seem to be even at our doors, nor should we wonder to see greater judgments still follow, both a famine of bread and of the

Word of the Lord, the sorest of all judgments. We have been often warned already, but instead of being humbled and reformed, we seem as a nation to be more hardened, and to wax worse and worse. Earthquakes and the murrain are perhaps forgotten by us, and hence we are more abandoned to wickedness than before. Because the Lord is long-suffering and slow to anger, multitudes presume to continue and harden themselves in sin. Thus, because judgment against an evil work is not executed speedily, the hearts of the sons of men are fully set in them to do evil (Eccles 8.11). But the longer the storm of God's wrath is in gathering, the heavier will it be when it comes: When I begin, saith God, I will also make an end. If mercies and goodness will not soften and win men to repentance, judgments and wrath will consume and destroy them; and justly may the heaviest of God's judgments be expected upon this dry tree of Great Britain.

With regard to the churches, it seems as if the Lord is about to sift and try, and purge them also in a way of judgment. Errors the most dangerous and subtle have spread exceedingly amongst us: and professors in general appear to be too remiss and negligent both in doctrine and practice. But if you would not be carried away with the torrent of error, oppose it with all diligence and steadfastness: for indeed, if you do not oppose error of every kind, it will gain upon you, and 'tis a sign also that in heart you secretly approve of it. Do you not, my Christian friends, find it necessary constantly to watch and pray, resist and fight against your own corruptions, that they may not lord it over you? so must you also watch and fight against those errors in doctrine which tend to lead you from Christ to proud self, from God's grace to man's free will, and conse-

[67]

quently will weaken your obligations to holiness, and so both indispose and disable you for the practice of it; for if you hold not fast sound doctrine, you will not long continue in an holy practice. Wherefore, fight the good fight of faith, lay hold on eternal life.

Be ye followers of God as dear children, and walk in love. True Christian love is undoubtedly the end of the commandment, the fulfilling of the law, and the certain evidence of grace, and of sound conversion to God; but see that this is of the right kind, for men nowadays call things by wrong names. They call that grace and righteousness which is not so. Thus, they put bitter for sweet and sweet for bitter. See then that your love be truly evangelical, i.e. for Christ's sake, and for the truth's sake only: for though in other respects a person may and ought to love his neighbour, yet this alone is that love which evidences a man's true conversion. This love is not confined to any party, name, or denomination whatever, but to all that know God, and love the Lord Jesus Christ in sincerity. So far as any one appears to have Christ formed in him, so far, if I am a Christian, I do and cannot but love him. But 'tis not man, but the image of Christ, that we love in any one after an holy, Christian manner. Follow therefore after charity. But take heed that no man deceive you with the name and sound of charity, candour and benevolence, instead of the thing itself. Many borrow these names to cover their secret designs but leave the grace behind them. The Arians and Socinians do this: they cry up meekness, charity, gentleness and benevolence. Thus they throw the dust of charity in our face, but 'tis only to put out our eyes, that we may not discern and reject their heresies: and this appears to be the manner of all in the wide scheme, who settle upon the free-will bottom: some of these deny the Deity and Godhead of Christ; some go so far as even to assert that his blood is of no efficacy for the expiating of our sins. The Lord keep you and me from such pernicious errors! I beseech you therefore, my brethren, to follow after that love, which makes continually for your mutual peace and edification, according to Christ Jesus.

6: The Scripture doctrine of election and predestination as we believe and preach it, is no discouragement to sinners, no bar to any one's conversion: for our warrant to come to Christ, is not God's secret decree and purpose concerning us; but his inviting, calling and commanding us in his Word to repent and believe on Christ. No one indeed can prove, or know his election, but by his conversion to God, and obeying the Gospel. They that believe aright do not believe in Christ from the consideration of their being elected, but from the consideration of their being lost sinners, whom Christ came to seek and to save. Neither do they who disobey the Gospel, reject Christ and his salvation from the consideration of their being reprobated, but because they love darkness rather than light, and voluntarily of their own free will choose the way that leadeth unto death. Nor will any one be condemned at the last day, because God, in righteousness, sovereignly passed him by, and did not elect him in Christ, but because he would not obey God and come unto Christ that he might have life. Neither are any impelled, and forcibly wrought upon against their will, either in rejecting or embracing the Gospel, but God leaves the reprobate to their own free choice, which is to sin always, but he makes his elect willing to come to Christ, by convincing them of their sin and danger in a state of nature, and shewing them Christ as the only way of safety, and peace with him: hence they freely and heartily come to

Christ, and lay hold on him by faith, that they might be saved. But they who do thus believe on the Son of God, turning to the Lord with their whole hearts, evidence thereby their election in Christ; for all true believers are God's elect; and this their believing is the fruit and effect of it. On the other hand, they that willingly continue in sin and unbelief unto the last, do thereby prove themselves not to be of the number of God's elect, but of them whom he hath justly reprobated.

Let none of you therefore, through ignorance, stumble at this doctrine, but be persuaded to come to Christ, and you shall be saved. All your sins of whatever kind, or degree, shall be forgiven you for his Name's sake, and he will assuredly bring you safe to his eternal glory: you have his own words for it, for 'whoso cometh unto me', saith Christ, 'I will in no wise cast out'; and 'whosoever believeth on him shall not perish, but have everlasting life'. If the greatest preacher upon earth, or an angel from heaven, were to tell any one of you, that you are not elected, and that although you should come to Christ he would not receive and save you, but reject and spurn you from him, believe him not; for God that cannot lie hath said, 'Whosoever believeth in him shall not be ashamed'. And he himself hath said, as you heard above, that if you come to him, he will in no wise cast you out: hence the Gospel is to be preached promiscuously to sinners, without distinction. Wherefore 'we pray you in Christ's stead be ye reconciled unto God, for he hath made him sin for us, who knew no sin, that we might be made the righteousness of God in him'. 'To him give all the prophets witness, that through his Name, whosoever believeth in him shall receive remission of sins.'

Finally, let us be followers of the dear Mr Whitefield as he was of Christ, not turning to the right hand or to the left, that we also, being followers of them who through faith and patience inherit the promise, may ere long be numbered with them, and inherit everlasting life; where, in a far more exalted manner, we shall ascribe the whole of our salvation unto God and unto the Lamb; to whom be glory for ever. AMEN.

SERMONS

THE METHOD OF GRACE

They have healed also the hurt of the daughter of my
people slightly, saying, Peace, peace, when there is no
peace. *Jer* 6.14

As God can send a nation or people no greater blessing
than to give them faithful, sincere, and upright ministers,
so the greatest curse that God can possibly send upon a
people in this world, is to give them over to blind, unregenerate, carnal, lukewarm, and unskilled guides. And yet, in
all ages, we find that there have been many wolves in
sheep's clothing, many that daubed with untempered mor-
tar, that prophesied smoother things than God did allow.
As it was formerly, so it is now; there are many that corrupt the Word of God and deal deceitfully with it. It was so
in a special manner in the prophet Jeremiah's time; and
he, faithful to his Lord, faithful to that God who employed
him, did not fail from time to time to open his mouth
against them, and to bear a noble testimony to the honour
of that God in whose name he from time to time spake. If
you will read his prophecy, you will find that none spake
more against such ministers than Jeremiah, and here
especially in the chapter out of which the text is taken, he
speaks very severely against them – he charges them with
several crimes; particularly, he charges them with covetousness: 'For', says he in the 13th verse, 'from the least of
them even to the greatest of them, every one is given to

covetousness; and from the prophet even unto the priest, every one dealeth falsely'. And then, in the words of the text, in a more special manner, he exemplifies how they had dealt falsely, how they had behaved treacherously to poor souls: says he, 'They have healed also the hurt of the daughter of my people slightly, saying, Peace, peace, when there is no peace'. The prophet, in the name of God, had been denouncing war against the people, he had been telling them that their house should be left desolate, and that the Lord would certainly visit the land with war. 'Therefore', says he, in the 11th verse, 'I am full of the fury of the Lord; I am weary with holding in; I will pour it out upon the children abroad, and upon the assembly of young men together; for even the husband with the wife shall be taken, the aged with him that is full of days. And their houses shall be turned unto others, with their fields and wives together; for I will stretch out my hand upon the inhabitants of the land, saith the Lord.' The prophet gives a thundering message, that they might be terrified and have some convictions and inclinations to repent; but it seems that the false prophets, the false priests, went about stifling people's convictions, and when they were hurt or a little terrified, they were for daubing over the wound, telling them that Jeremiah was but an enthusiastic preacher, that there could be no such thing as war among them, and saying to people, Peace, peace, be still, when the prophet told them there was no peace. The words, then, refer primarily unto outward things, but I verily believe have also a further reference to the soul, and are to be referred to those false teachers, who, when people were under conviction of sin, when people were beginning to look towards heaven, were for stifling their convictions and telling them they were good enough before. And, indeed, people generally love to have it so; our hearts are exceedingly deceitful, and desperately wicked; none but the eternal God knows how treacherous they are. How many of us cry, Peace, peace, to our souls, when there is no peace! How many are there who are now settled upon their lees, that now think they are Christians, that now flatter themselves that they have an interest in Jesus Christ; whereas if we come to examine their experiences, we shall find that their peace is but a peace of the devil's making—it is not a peace of God's giving—it is not a peace that passeth human understanding. It is matter, therefore, of great importance, my dear hearers, to know whether we may speak peace to our hearts. We are all desirous of peace; peace is an unspeakable blessing; how can we live without peace? And, therefore, people from time to time must be taught how far they must go, and what must be wrought in them, before they can speak peace to their hearts. This is what I design at present, that I may deliver my soul, that I may be free from the blood of those to whom I preach—that I may not fail to declare the whole counsel of God. I shall, from the words of the text, endeavour to show you what you must undergo, and what must be wrought in you before you can speak peace to your hearts.

But before I come directly to this, give me leave to premise a caution or two. And the first is, that I take it for granted you believe religion to be an inward thing; you believe it to be a work in the heart, a work wrought in the soul by the power of the Spirit of God. If you do not believe this, you do not believe your Bibles. If you do not believe this, though you have got your Bibles in your hand, you hate the Lord Jesus Christ in your heart; for religion is everywhere represented in Scripture as the work of God in the heart. 'The kingdom of God is within us', says our Lord; and, 'He is not a Christian who is one outwardly; but he is a Christian who is one inwardly'. If any of you place religion in outward things, I shall not perhaps please you this morning; you will understand me no more when I speak of the work of God upon a poor sinner's heart, than if I were talking in an unknown tongue. I would further premise a caution, that I would by no means confine God to one way of acting. I would by no means say, that all persons, before they come to have a settled peace in their hearts, are obliged to undergo the same degrees of conviction. No; God has various ways of bringing his children home; his sacred Spirit bloweth when, and where, and how it listeth. But, however, I will venture to affirm this, that before ever you can speak peace to your heart, whether by shorter or longer continuance of your convictions, whether in a more pungent or in a more gentle way, you must undergo what I shall hereafter lay down in the following discourse.

First, then, before you can speak peace to your hearts, you must be made to see, made to feel, made to weep over, made to bewail, your actual transgressions against the law of God. According to the covenant of works, 'The soul that sinneth it shall die'; cursed is that man, be he what he may, that continueth not in all things that are written in the book of the law to do them. We are not only to do some things, but we are to do all things, and we are to continue so to do; so that the least deviation from the moral law, according to the covenant of works, whether in thought, word, or deed, deserves eternal death at the hand of God. And if one evil thought, if one evil word, if one evil action, deserves eternal damnation, how many hells, my friends, do every one of us deserve, whose whole lives have been one continued rebellion against God! Before ever, therefore, you can speak peace to your hearts, you must be brought to see, brought to believe, what a dreadful thing it is to depart from the living God. And now, my dear friends, examine your hearts, for I hope you came hither with a design to have your souls made better. Give me leave to ask you, in the presence of God, whether you know the time, and if you do not know exactly the time, do you know there was a time, when God wrote bitter things against you, when the arrows of the Almighty were within you? Was ever the remembrance of your sins grievous to you? Was the burden of your sins intolerable to your thoughts? Did you ever see that God's wrath might justly fall upon you, on account of your actual transgressions against God? Were you ever in all your life sorry for your sins? Could you ever say, My sins are gone over my head as a burden too heavy for me to bear? Did you ever experience any such thing as this? Did ever any such thing as this pass between God and your soul? If not, for Jesus Christ's sake, do not call yourselves Christians; you may speak peace to your hearts, but there is no peace. May the Lord awaken you, may the Lord convert you, may the Lord give you peace, if it be his will, before you go home!

But further: you may be convinced of your actual sins, so as to be made to tremble, and yet you may be strangers to Jesus Christ, you may have no true work of grace upon your hearts. Before ever, therefore, you can speak peace to your hearts, conviction must go deeper; you must not only be convinced of your actual transgressions against the law of God, but likewise of the foundation of all your transgressions. And what is that? I mean original sin, that

[79]

original corruption each of us brings into the world with us, which renders us liable to God's wrath and damnation. There are many poor souls that think themselves fine reasoners, yet they pretend to say there is no such thing as original sin; they will charge God with injustice in imputing Adam's sin to us; although we have got the mark of the beast and of the devil upon us, yet they tell us we are not born in sin. Let them look abroad into the world and see the disorders in it, and think, if they can, if this is the paradise in which God did put man. No! everything in the world is out of order. I have often thought, when I was abroad, that if there were no other argument to prove original sin, the rising of wolves and tigers against man, nay, the barking of a dog against us, is a proof of original sin. Tigers and lions durst not rise against us, if it were not for Adam's first sin; for when the creatures rise up against us, it is as much as to say, You have sinned against God, and we take up our Master's quarrel. If we look inwardly, we shall see enough of lusts, and man's temper contrary to the temper of God. There is pride, malice, and revenge, in all our hearts; and this temper cannot come from God; it comes from our first parent, Adam, who, after he fell from God, fell out of God into the devil. However, therefore, some people may deny this, yet when conviction comes, all carnal reasonings are battered down immediately and the poor soul begins to feel and see the fountain from which all the polluted streams do flow. When the sinner is first awakened, he begins to wonder — How came I to be so wicked? The Spirit of God then strikes in, and shows that he has no good thing in him by nature; then he sees that he is altogether gone out of the way, that he is altogether become abominable, and the poor creature is made to lie down at the foot of the throne of God, and to acknowledge that God would be just to damn him, just to cut him off, though he never had committed one actual sin in his life. Did you ever feel and experience this, any of you — to justify God in your damnation — to own that you are by nature children of wrath, and that God may justly cut you off, though you never actually had offended him in all your life? If you were ever truly convicted, if your hearts were ever truly cut, if self were truly taken out of you, you would be made to see and feel this. And if you have never felt the weight of original sin, do not call yourselves Christians. I am verily persuaded original sin is the greatest burden of a true convert; this ever grieves the regenerate soul, the sanctified soul. The indwelling of sin in the heart is the burden of a converted person; it is the burden of a true Christian. He continually cries out, 'O! who will deliver me from this body of death', this indwelling corruption in my heart? This is that which disturbs a poor soul most. And, therefore, if you never felt this inward corruption, if you never saw that God might justly curse you for it, indeed, my dear friends, you may speak peace to your hearts, but I fear, nay, I know, there is no true peace.

Further: before you can speak peace to your hearts, you must not only be troubled for the sins of your life, the sin of your nature, but likewise for the sins of your best duties and performances. When a poor soul is somewhat awakened by the terrors of the Lord, then the poor creature, being born under the covenant of works, flies directly to a covenant of works again. And as Adam and Eve hid themselves among the trees of the garden, and sewed fig leaves together to cover their nakedness, so the poor sinner, when awakened, flies to his duties and to his performances, to hide himself from

[81]

God, and goes to patch up a righteousness of his own. Says he, I will be mighty good now—I will reform—I will do all I can; and then certainly Jesus Christ will have mercy on me. But before you can speak peace to your heart, you must be brought to see that God may damn you for the best prayer you ever put up; you must be brought to see that all your duties—all your righteousness—as the prophet elegantly expresses it—put them all together, are so far from recommending you to God, are so far from being any motive and inducement to God to have mercy on your poor soul, that he will see them to be filthy rags, a menstruous cloth—that God hates them, and cannot away with them, if you bring them to him in order to recommend you to his favour. My dear friends, what is there in our performances to recommend us unto God? Our persons are in an unjustified state by nature, we deserve to be damned ten thousand times over; and what must our performances be? We can do no good thing by nature: 'They that are in the flesh cannot please God.' You may do things materially good, but you cannot do a thing formally and rightly good; because nature cannot act above itself. It is impossible that a man who is unconverted can act for the glory of God; he cannot do anything in faith, and 'whatsoever is not of faith is sin'. After we are renewed, yet we are renewed but in part, indwelling sin continues in us, there is a mixture of corruption in every one of our duties; so that after we are converted, were Jesus Christ only to accept us according to our works, our works would damn us, for we cannot put up a prayer but it is far from that perfection which the moral law requireth. I do not know what you may think, but I can say that I cannot pray but I sin—I cannot preach to you or any others but I sin—I can do nothing without sin; and, as one expresseth it, my repentance wants to be repented of, and my tears to be washed in the precious blood of my dear Redeemer. Our best duties are as so many splendid sins. Before you can speak peace in your heart, you must not only be made sick of your original and actual sin, but you must be made sick of your righteousness, of all your duties and performances. There must be a deep conviction before you can be brought out of your self-righteousness; it is the last idol taken out of our heart. The pride of our heart will not let us submit to the righteousness of Jesus Christ. But if you never felt that you had no righteousness of your own, if you never felt the deficiency of your own righteousness, you cannot come to Jesus Christ. There are a great many now who may say, Well, we believe all this; but there is a great difference betwixt talking and feeling. Did you ever feel the want of a dear Redeemer? Did you ever feel the want of Jesus Christ, upon the account of the deficiency of your own righteousness? And can you now say from your heart, Lord, thou mayst justly damn me for the best duties that ever I did perform? If you are not thus brought out of self, you may speak peace to yourselves, but yet there is no peace.

But then, before you can speak peace to your souls, there is one particular sin you must be greatly troubled for, and yet I fear there are few of you think what it is; it is the reigning, the damning sin of the Christian world, and yet the Christian world seldom or never think of it. And pray what is that? It is what most of you think you are not guilty of—and that is, the sin of unbelief. Before you can speak peace to your heart, you must be troubled for the unbelief of your heart. But, can it be supposed that any of you are unbelievers here in this church-yard, that are born in Scotland, in a reformed country, that go to church every Sabbath? Can any of you that receive the sacrament once a year—O that it were administered oftener!—can it be supposed that you who had tokens for the sacrament, that you who keep up family prayer, that any of you do not believe in the Lord Jesus Christ? I appeal to your own hearts, if you would not think me uncharitable, if I doubted whether any of you believed in Christ; and yet, I fear upon examination, we should find that most of you have not so much faith in the Lord Jesus Christ as the devil himself. I am persuaded the devil believes more of the Bible than most of us do. He believes the divinity of Jesus Christ; that is more than many who call themselves Christians do; nay, he believes and trembles, and that is more than thousands amongst us do. My friends, we mistake a historical faith for a true faith, wrought in the heart by the Spirit of God. You fancy you believe, because you believe there is such a book as we call the Bible—because you go to church; all this you may do, and have no true faith in Christ. Merely to believe there was such a person as Christ, merely to believe there is a book called the Bible, will do you no good, more than to believe there was such a man as Cæsar or Alexander the Great. The Bible is a sacred depository. What thanks have we to give to God for these lively oracles! But yet we may have these, and not believe in the Lord Jesus Christ. My dear friends, there must be a principle wrought in the heart by the Spirit of the living God. Did I ask you how long it is since you believed in Jesus Christ, I suppose most of you would tell me, you believed in Jesus Christ as long as ever you remember—you never did misbelieve. Then, you could not give me a better proof that you never yet believed in Jesus Christ, unless you were sanctified early, as from the womb; for, they that otherwise believe in Christ know there was a time when they did not believe in Jesus Christ. You say you love God with all your heart, soul, and strength. If I were to ask you how long it is since you loved God, you would say, As long as you can remember; you never hated God, you know no time when there was enmity in your heart against God. Then, unless you were sanctified very early, you never loved God in your life. My dear friends, I am more particular in this, because it is a most deceitful delusion, whereby so many people are carried away, that they believe already. Therefore, it is remarked of Mr Marshall, giving account of his experiences, that he had been working for life, and he had ranged all his sins under the ten commandments, and then coming to a minister, asked him the reason why he could not get peace. The minister looked at his catalogue. Away, says he, I do not find one word of the sin of unbelief in all your catalogue. It is the peculiar work of the Spirit of God to convince us of our unbelief – that we have got no faith. Says Jesus Christ, 'I will send the Comforter; and when he is come, he will reprove the world' of the sin of unbelief; 'of sin', says Christ, 'because they believe not on me'. Now, my dear friends, did God ever show you that you had no faith? Were you ever made to bewail a hard heart of unbelief? Was it ever the language of your heart, Lord, give me faith; Lord, enable me to lay hold on thee; Lord, enable me to call thee *my* Lord and *my* God? Did Jesus Christ ever convince you in this manner? Did he ever convince you of your inability to close with Christ, and make you to cry out to God to give you faith? If not, do not speak peace to your heart. May the Lord awaken you, and give you true, solid peace before you go hence and be no more!

Once more then: before you can speak peace to your heart, you must not only be convinced of your actual and original sin, the sins of your own righteousness, the sin of unbelief, but you must be enabled to lay hold upon the perfect righteousness, the all-sufficient righteousness, of the Lord Jesus Christ; you must lay hold by faith on the righteousness of Jesus Christ, and then you shall have peace. 'Come', says Jesus, 'unto me, all ye that are weary and heavy laden, and I will give you rest.' This speaks encouragement to all that are weary and heavy laden; but the promise of rest is made to them only upon their coming and believing, and taking him to be their God and their all. Before we can ever have peace with God, we must be justified by faith through our Lord Jesus Christ, we must be enabled to apply Christ to our hearts, we must have Christ brought home to our souls, so as his righteousness may be made our righteousness, so as his merits may be imputed to our souls. My dear friends, were you ever married to Jesus Christ? Did Jesus Christ ever give himself to you? Did you ever close with Christ by a lively faith, so as to feel Christ in your hearts, so as to hear him speaking peace to your souls? Did peace ever flow in upon your hearts like a river? Did you ever feel that peace that Christ spoke to his disciples? I pray God he may come and speak peace to you. These things you must experience. I am now talking of the invisible realities of another world, of inward religion, of the work of God upon a poor sinner's heart. I am now talking of a matter of great importance, my dear hearers; you are all concerned in it, your souls are concerned in it, your eternal salvation is concerned in it. You may be all at peace, but perhaps the devil has lulled you asleep into a carnal lethargy and security, and will endeavour to keep you there, till he get you to hell, and there you will be awakened; but it will be dreadful to be awakened and find yourselves so fearfully mistaken, when the great gulf is fixed, when you will be calling to all eternity for a drop of water to cool your tongue, and shall not obtain it.

Give me leave, then, to address myself to several sorts of persons; and O may God, of his infinite mercy, bless the application! There are some of you perhaps can say, Through grace we can go along with you. Blessed be God, we have been convinced of our actual sins, we have been convinced of original sin, we have been convinced of self-righteousness, we have felt the bitterness of unbelief, and through grace we have closed with Jesus Christ; we can speak peace to our hearts, because God hath spoken peace to us. Can you say so? Then I will salute you, as the angels did the women the first day of the week, All hail! fear not ye, my dear brethren, you are happy souls; you may lie down and be at peace indeed, for God hath given you peace; you may be content under all the dispensations of providence, for nothing can happen to you now, but what shall be the effect of God's love to your soul; you need not fear what fightings may be without, seeing there is peace within. Have you closed with Christ? Is God your friend? Is Christ your friend? Then, look up with comfort; all is yours, and you are Christ's, and Christ is God's. Everything shall work together for your good; the very hairs of your head are numbered; he that toucheth you, toucheth the apple of God's eye. But then, my dear friends, beware of resting on your first conversion. You that are young believers in Christ, you should be looking out for fresh discoveries of the Lord Jesus Christ every moment; you must not build upon your past experiences, you must not build upon a work within you, but always come out of yourselves to the righteousness of Jesus Christ without you; you must be always coming as poor sinners to draw water out of the wells of salvation; you must be forgetting the things that are behind, and be continually pressing forward to the things that are before. My dear friends, you must keep up a tender, close walk with the Lord Jesus Christ. There are many of us who lose our peace by our untender walk; something or other gets in betwixt Christ and us, and we fall into darkness; something or other steals our hearts from God, and this grieves the Holy Ghost, and the Holy Ghost leaves us to ourselves. Let me, therefore, exhort you that have got peace with God, to take care that you do not lose this peace. It is true, if you are once in Christ, you cannot finally fall from God: 'There is no condemnation to them that are in Christ Jesus'; but if you cannot fall finally, you may fall foully, and may go with broken bones all your days. Take care of backslidings; for Jesus Christ's sake, do not grieve the Holy Ghost – you may never recover your comfort while you live. O take care of going a gadding and wandering from God, after you have closed with Jesus Christ. My dear friends, I have paid dear for backsliding. Our hearts are so cursedly wicked, that if you take not care, if you do not keep up a constant watch, your wicked hearts will deceive you, and draw you aside. It will be sad to be under the scourge of a correcting Father; witness the visitations of Job, David, and other saints in Scripture. Let me, therefore, exhort you that have got peace to keep a close walk with Christ. I am grieved with the loose walk of those that are Christians, that have had discoveries of Jesus Christ; there is so little difference betwixt them and other people, that I scarce know which is the true Christian. Christians are afraid to speak for God – they run down with the stream; if they come into worldly company, they will talk of the world as if they were in their element; this you would not do when you had the first discoveries of Christ's love; you could talk then of Christ's love for ever, when the candle of the Lord shined upon your soul. That time has been when you had something to say for your dear Lord; but now you can go into company and hear others speaking about the world bold enough, and you are afraid of being laughed at if you speak for Jesus Christ. A great many people have grown conformists now in the worst sense of the word; they will cry out against the ceremonies of the church, as they may justly do; but then you are mighty fond of ceremonies in your behaviour; you will conform to the world, which is a great deal worse. Many will stay till the devil bring up new fashions. Take care, then, not to be conformed to the world. What have Christians to do with the world? Christians should be singularly good, bold for their Lord, that all who are with you may take notice that you have been with Jesus. I would exhort you to come to a settlement in Jesus Christ, so as to have a continual abiding of God in your heart. We go a-building on our faith of adherence, and lose our comfort; but we should be growing up to a faith of assurance, to know that we are God's, and so walk in the comfort of the Holy Ghost and be edified. Jesus Christ is now much wounded in the house of his friends. Excuse me in being particular; for, my friends, it grieves me more that Jesus Christ should be wounded by his friends than by his enemies. We cannot expect anything else from Deists; but for such as have felt his power, to fall away, for them not to walk agreeably to the vocation wherewith they are called – by these means we bring our Lord's religion into contempt, to be a byword among the heathen. For Christ's sake, if you know Christ keep close by him; if God have spoken peace, O keep that peace by looking up to Jesus Christ every moment. Such as have got peace with God, if you are under trials, fear not, all things shall work for your good; if you are under temptations, fear not, if he has spoken peace to your hearts, all these things shall be for your good.

But what shall I say to you that have got no peace with God? — and these are, perhaps, the most of this congregation: it makes me weep to think of it. Most of you, if you examine your hearts, must confess that God never yet spoke peace to you; you are children of the devil, if Christ is not in you, if God has not spoken peace to your heart. Poor soul! what a cursed condition are you in. I would not be in your case for ten thousand, thousand worlds. Why? You are just hanging over hell. What peace can you have when God is your enemy, when the wrath of God is abiding upon your poor soul? Awake, then, you that are sleeping in a false peace, awake, ye carnal professors, ye hypocrites that go to church, receive the sacrament, read your Bibles, and never felt the power of God upon your hearts; you that are formal professors, you that are baptized heathens; awake, awake, and do not rest on a false bottom. Blame me not for addressing myself to you; indeed, it is out of love to your souls. I see you are lingering in your Sodom, and wanting to stay there; but I come to you as the angel did to Lot, to take you by the hand. Come away, my dear brethren — fly, fly, fly for your lives to Jesus Christ, fly to a bleeding God, fly to a throne of grace; and beg of God to break your hearts, beg of God to convince you of your actual sins, beg of God to convince you of your original sin, beg of God to convince you of your self-righteousness — beg of God to give you faith, and to enable you to close with Jesus Christ. O you that are secure, I must be a son of thunder to you, and O that God may awaken you, though it be with thunder; it is out of love, indeed, that I speak to you. I know by sad experience what it is to be lulled asleep with a false peace; long was I lulled asleep, long did I think myself a Christian, when I knew nothing of the Lord Jesus Christ. I went perhaps farther than many of you do; I used to fast twice a-week, I used to pray sometimes nine times a-day, I used to receive the sacrament constantly every Lord's-day; and yet I knew nothing of Jesus Christ in my heart, I knew not that I must be a new creature – I knew nothing of inward religion in my soul. And perhaps, many of you may be deceived as I, poor creature, was; and, therefore, it is out of love to you indeed, that I speak to you. O if you do not take care, a form of religion will destroy your soul; you will rest in it, and will not come to Jesus Christ at all; whereas, these things are only the means, and not the end of religion; Christ is the end of the law for righteousness to all that believe. O, then, awake, you that are settled on your lees; awake you Church professors; awake you that have got a name to live, that are rich and think you want nothing, not considering that you are poor, and blind, and naked; I counsel you to come and buy of Jesus Christ gold, white raiment, and eye-salve. But I hope there are some that are a little wounded; I hope God does not intend to let me preach in vain; I hope God will reach some of your precious souls, and awaken some of you out of your carnal security; I hope there are some who are willing to come to Christ, and beginning to think that they have been building upon a false foundation. Perhaps the devil may strike in, and bid you despair of mercy; but fear not, what I have been speaking to you is only out of love to you – is only to awaken you, and let you see your danger. If any of you are willing to be reconciled to God, God the Father, Son, and Holy Ghost, is willing to be reconciled to you. O then, though you have no peace as yet, come away to Jesus Christ; he is our peace, he is our peace-maker — he has made peace betwixt God and offending man. Would you have peace with God? Away, then, to God through Jesus Christ, who has purchased peace; the Lord Jesus has shed his heart's blood for this. He died for this; he rose again for this; he ascended into the highest heaven, and is now interceding at the right hand of God. Perhaps you think there will be no peace for you. Why so? Because you are sinners? because you have crucified Christ — you have put him to open shame — you have trampled under foot the blood of the Son of God? What of all this? Yet there is peace for you. Pray, what did Jesus Christ say of his disciples, when he came to them the first day of the week? The first word he said was, 'Peace be unto you'; he showed them his hands and his side, and said, 'Peace be unto you'. It is as much as if he had said, Fear not, my disciples; see my hands and my feet how they have been pierced for your sake; therefore fear not. How did Christ speak to his disciples? 'Go tell my brethren, and tell broken-hearted Peter in particular, that Christ is risen, that he is ascended unto his Father and your Father, to his God and your God.' And after Christ rose from the dead, he came preaching peace, with an olive branch of peace, like Noah's dove: 'My peace I leave with you.' Who were they? They were enemies of Christ as well as we, they were deniers of Christ once as well as we. Perhaps some of you have backslidden and lost your peace, and you think you deserve no peace; and no more you do. But, then, God will heal your backslidings, he will love you freely. As for you that are wounded, if you are made willing to come to Christ, come away. Perhaps some of you want to dress yourselves in your duties, that are but rotten rags. No, you had better come naked as you are, for you must throw aside your rags, and come in your blood. Some of you may say, We would come, but we have got a hard heart. But you will never get it made soft till ye come to Christ; he will take away the heart of stone, and give you an heart of flesh; he will speak peace to your souls; though ye have betrayed him, yet he will be your peace. Shall I prevail upon any of you this morning to come to Jesus Christ? There is a great multitude of souls here; how shortly must you all die, and go to judgment! Even before night, or to-morrow's night, some of you may be laid out for this kirk-yard. And how will you do if you be not at peace with God – if the Lord Jesus Christ has not spoken peace to your heart? If God speak not peace to you here, you will be damned for ever. I must not flatter you, my dear friends; I will deal sincerely with your souls. Some of you may think I carry things too far. But, indeed, when you come to judgment, you will find what I say is true, either to your eternal damnation or comfort. May God influence your hearts to come to him! I am not willing to go away without persuading you. I cannot be persuaded but God may make use of me as a means of persuading some of you to come to the Lord Jesus Christ. O did you but feel the peace which they have that love the Lord Jesus Christ! 'Great peace have they', say the psalmist, 'that love thy law; nothing shall offend them.' But there is no peace to the wicked. I know what it is to live a life of sin; I was obliged to sin in order to stifle conviction. And I am sure this is the way many of you take; If you get into company, you drive off conviction. But you had better go to the bottom at once; it must be done – your wound must be searched, or you must be damned. If it were a matter of indifference, I would not speak one word about it. But you will be damned without Christ. He is the way, he is the truth, and the life. I cannot think you should go to hell without Christ. How can you dwell with everlasting burnings? How can you abide the thought of living with the devil for ever? Is it not better to have some soul-trouble here, than to be sent to hell by Jesus Christ hereafter? What is hell, but to be absent from Christ? If there were no other hell, that would be hell enough. It will be hell to be tormented with the devil for ever. Get acquaintance with God, then, and be at peace. I beseech you, as a poor worthless ambassador of Jesus Christ, that you would be reconciled to God. My business this morning, the first day of the week, is to tell you that Christ is willing to be reconciled to you. Will any of you be reconciled to Jesus Christ? Then, he will forgive you all your sins, he will blot out all your transgressions. But if you will go on and rebel against Christ, and stab him daily—if you will go on and abuse Jesus Christ, the wrath of God you must expect will fall upon you. God will not be mocked; that which a man soweth, that shall he also reap. And if you will not be at peace with God, God will not be at peace with you. Who can stand before God when he is angry? It is a dreadful thing to fall into the hands of an angry God. When the people came to apprehend Christ, they fell to the ground when Jesus said, 'I am he'. And if they could not bear the sight of Christ when clothed with the rags of mortality, how will they bear the sight of him when he is on his Father's throne? Methinks I see the poor wretches dragged out of their graves by the devil; methinks I see them trembling, crying out to the hills and rocks to cover them. But the devil will say, Come, I will take you away; and then they shall stand trembling before the judgment-seat of Christ. They shall appear before him to see him once, and hear him pronounce that irrevocable sentence, 'Depart from me, ye cursed'. Methinks I hear the poor creatures saying, Lord, if we must be damned, let some angel pronounce the sentence. No, the God of love, Jesus Christ, will pronounce it. Will ye not believe this? Do not think I am talking at random, but agreeably to the Scriptures of truth. If you do not, then show yourselves men, and this morning go away with full resolution, in the strength of God, to cleave to Christ. And may you have no rest in your souls till you rest in Jesus Christ! I could still go on, for it is sweet to talk of Christ. Do you not long for the time when you shall have new bodies – when they shall be immortal, and made like Christ's glorious body? and then they will talk of Jesus Christ for evermore. But it is time, perhaps, for you to go and prepare for your respective worship, and I would not hinder any of you. My design is, to bring poor sinners to Jesus Christ. O that God may bring some of you to himself! May the Lord Jesus now dismiss you with his blessing, and may the dear Redeemer convince you that are unawakened, and turn the wicked from the evil of their way! And may the love of God, that passeth all understanding, fill your hearts. Grant this, O Father, for Christ's sake; to whom, with thee and the blessed Spirit, be all honour and glory, now and for evermore. Amen.

CHRIST THE BELIEVER'S WISDOM
RIGHTEOUSNESS, SANCTIFICATION AND
REDEMPTION

But of him are ye in Christ Jesus, who of God is
made unto us wisdom, and righteousness, and sanctification,
and redemption. 1 *Cor* 1.30

Of all the verses in the book of God, this which I have now
read to you, is, I believe, one of the most comprehensive:
what glad tidings does it bring to believers! what precious
privileges are they herein invested with! how are they here
led to the fountain of them all, I mean, the love, the everlasting love of God the Father! 'Of him are ye in Christ
Jesus, who of God is made unto us wisdom, righteousness,
sanctification, and redemption.'

Without referring you to the context, I shall from the
words,

First, Point out to you the fountain, from which all those
blessings flow, that the elect of God partake of in Jesus
Christ, 'Who of God is made unto us'. And,

Secondly, I shall consider what these blessings are, 'Wisdom, righteousness, sanctification, and redemption'.

First, I would point out to you the fountain, from which
all those blessings flow, that the elect of God partake of in
Jesus, 'who of God is made unto us', the Father, he it is who
is spoken of here. Not as though Jesus Christ was not God
also; but God the Father is the fountain of the Deity; and
if we consider Jesus Christ acting as Mediator, God the
Father is greater than he; there was an eternal contract

between the Father and the Son: 'I have made a covenant with my chosen, and I have sworn unto David my servant'; now David was a type of Christ, with whom the Father made a covenant, that if he would obey and suffer, and make himself a sacrifice for sin, he should 'see his seed, he should prolong his days, and the pleasure of the Lord should prosper in his hands'. This compact our Lord refers to, in that glorious prayer recorded in the 17th chapter of John; and therefore he prays for, or rather demands with a full assurance, all that were given to him by the Father: 'Father, I will that they also whom thou hast given me, be with me where I am.' For this same reason, the apostle breaks out into praises of God, even the Father of our Lord Jesus Christ; for he loved the elect with an everlasting love, or, as our Lord expresses it, 'before the foundation of the world'; and, therefore, to shew them to whom they were beholden for their salvation, our Lord, in the 25th of Matthew, represents himself saying, 'Come, ye blessed children of my Father, receive the kingdom prepared for you from the foundation of the world'. And thus, in reply to the mother of Zebedee's children, he says, 'It is not mine to give, but it shall be given to them for whom it is prepared of the Father'. The apostle therefore, when here speaking of the Christian's privileges, lest they should sacrifice to their own drag, or think their salvation was owing to their own faithfulness, or improvement of their own free-will, reminds them to look back on the everlasting love of God the Father; 'who of God is made unto us', etc.

Would to God this point of doctrine was considered more, and people were more studious of the covenant of redemption between the Father and the Son! we should not then have so much disputing against the doctrine of election, or hear it condemned (even by good men) as a doctrine of devils. For my own part, I cannot see how true humbleness of mind can be attained without a knowledge of it; and though I will not say, that every one who denies election is a bad man, yet I will say, with that sweet singer, Mr Trail, it is a very bad sign: such a one, whoever he be, I think cannot truly know himself; for, if we deny election, we must, partly at least, glory in ourselves; but our redemption is so ordered, that no flesh should glory in the Divine presence; and hence it is, that the pride of man opposes this doctrine, because, according to this doctrine, and no other, 'he that glories, must glory only in the Lord'. But what shall I say? Election is a mystery that shines with such resplendent brightness, that, to make use of the words of one who has drunk deeply of electing love, it dazzles the weak eyes even of some of God's dear children; however, though they know it not, all the blessings they receive, all the privileges they do or will enjoy, through Jesus Christ, flow from the everlasting love of God the Father: 'But of him are you in Christ Jesus, who of God is made unto us, wisdom, righteousness, sanctification, and redemption.'

Secondly, I come to shew what these blessings are, which are here, through Christ, made over to the elect. And,

1: *First*, Christ is made to them *Wisdom*; but wherein does true wisdom consist? Were I to ask some of you, perhaps you would say, in indulging the lust of the flesh, and saying to your souls, eat, drink, and be merry: but this is only the wisdom of brutes; they have as good a gust and relish for sensual pleasures, as the greatest epicure on earth. Others would tell me, true wisdom consisted in adding house to house, and field to field, and calling lands after their own names: but this cannot be true wisdom; for riches often take to themselves wings, and fly away, like an eagle towards heaven. Even wisdom itself assures us, 'that a man's life doth not consist in the abundance of the things which he possesses'; vanity, vanity, all these things are vanity; for, if riches leave not the owner, the owners must soon leave them; 'for rich men must also die, and leave their riches for others'; their riches cannot procure them redemption from the grave, whither we are all hastening apace.

But perhaps you despise riches and pleasure, and therefore place wisdom in the knowledge of books: but it is possible for you to tell the numbers of the stars, and call them all by their names, and yet be mere fools; learned men are not always wise; nay, our common learning, so much cried up, makes men only so many accomplished fools; to keep you therefore no longer in suspense, and withal to humble you, I will send you to a heathen to school, to learn what true wisdom is: 'Know thyself', was a saying of one of the wise men of Greece; this is certainly true wisdom, and this is that wisdom spoken of in the text, and which Jesus Christ is made to all elect sinners — they are made to know themselves, so as not to think more highly of themselves than they ought to think. Before, they were darkness; now, they are light in the Lord; and in that light they see their own darkness; they now bewail themselves as fallen creatures by nature, dead in trespasses and sins, sons and heirs of hell, and children of wrath; they now see that all their righteousnesses are but as filthy rags; that there is no health in their souls; that they are poor and miserable, blind and naked; and that there is no name given under heaven, whereby they can be saved, but that of Jesus Christ. They see the necessity of closing with a Saviour, and behold the wisdom of God in appointing him to be a Saviour; they are also made willing to accept of salvation upon our Lord's own terms, and receive him as their all in all: thus Christ is made to them wisdom.

2: *Secondly, Righteousness*, 'Who of God is made unto us, wisdom, righteousness': Christ's whole personal righteousness is made over to, and accounted theirs. They are enabled to lay hold on Christ by faith, and God the Father blots out their transgressions, as with a thick cloud: their sins and their iniquities he remembers no more; they are made the righteousness of God in Christ Jesus, 'who is the end of the law for righteousness to every one that believeth'. In one sense, God now sees no sin in them; the whole covenant of works is fulfilled in them; they are actually justified, acquitted, and looked upon as righteous in the sight of God; they are perfectly accepted in the beloved; they are complete in him; the flaming sword of God's wrath, which before moved every way, is now removed, and free access given to the tree of life; they are enabled to reach out the arm of faith, and pluck, and live for evermore. Hence it is that the apostle, under a sense of this blessed privilege, breaks out into this triumphant language; 'It is Christ that justifies, who is he that condemns?' Does sin condemn? Christ's righteousness delivers believers from the guilt of it: Christ is their Saviour, and is become a propitiation for their sins: who therefore shall lay any thing to the charge of God's elect? Does the law condemn? By having Christ's righteousness imputed to them, they are dead to the law, as a covenant of works; Christ has fulfilled it for them, and in their stead. Does death threaten them? They need not fear: the sting of death is sin, the strength of sin is the law; but God has given them the victory by imputing to them the righteousness of the Lord Jesus.

And what a privilege is here! Well might the angels at the birth of Christ say to the humble shepherds, 'Behold, I bring you glad tidings of great joy'; unto you that believe in Christ 'a Saviour is born'. And well may angels rejoice at the conversion of poor sinners; for the Lord is their righteousness; they have peace with God through faith in Christ's blood, and shall never enter into condemnation. O believers! (for this discourse is intended in a special manner for you) lift up your heads; 'rejoice in the Lord always; again I say, rejoice'. Christ is made to you, of God, righteousness, what then should you fear? You are made the righteousness of God in him; you may be called, 'The Lord our righteousness'. Of what then should you be afraid? What shall separate you henceforward from the love of Christ? 'Shall tribulation, or distress, or persecution, or famine, or nakedness, or peril, or sword? No, I am persuaded, neither death, nor life, nor angels, nor principalities, nor powers, nor things present, nor things to come, nor height, nor depth, nor any other creature, shall be able to separate you from the love of God, which is in Christ Jesus our Lord', who of God is made unto you righteousness.

This is a glorious privilege, but this is only the beginning of the happiness of believers: For,

3 : *Thirdly*, Christ is not only made to them righteousness, but sanctification; by sanctification, I do not mean a bare hypocritical attendance on outward ordinances, though rightly informed Christians will think it their duty and privilege constantly to attend on all outward ordinances. Nor do I mean by sanctification a bare outward reformation, and a few transient convictions, or a little legal sorrow; for all this an unsanctified man may have; but, by sanctification I mean a total renovation of the whole man: by the righte-

[101]

ousness of Christ, believers come legally, by sanctification they are made spiritually, alive; by the one they are entitled to, by the other they are made meet for, glory. They are sanctified, therefore, throughout, in spirit, soul, and body.

Their understandings, which were dark before, now become light in the Lord; and their wills, before contrary to, now become one with the will of God; their affections are now set on things above; their memory is now filled with divine things; their natural consciences are now enlightened; their members, which were before instruments of uncleanness, and of iniquity into iniquity, are now new creatures; 'old things are passed away, all things are become new', in their hearts: sin has now no longer dominion over them; they are freed from the power, though not the indwelling and being, of it; they are holy both in heart and life, in all manner of conversation; they are made partakers of a divine nature, and from Jesus Christ, they receive grace; and every grace that is in Christ, is copied and transcribed into their souls; they are transformed into his likeness; he is formed within them; they dwell in him, and he in them; they are led by the Spirit, and bring forth the fruits thereof; they know that Christ is their Emmanuel, God with and in them; they are living temples of the Holy Ghost. And therefore, being a holy habitation unto the Lord, the whole Trinity dwells and walks in them; even here, they sit together with Christ in heavenly places, and are vitally united to him, their Head, by a living faith; their Redeemer, their Maker, is their husband; they are flesh of his flesh, bone of his bone; they talk, they walk with him, as a man talketh and walketh with his friend; in short, they are one with Christ, even as Jesus Christ and the Father are one.

Thus is Christ made to believers sanctification. And O

what a privilege is this! to be changed from beasts into saints, and from a devilish, to be made partakers of a divine nature; to be translated from the kingdom of Satan, into the kingdom of God's dear Son! to put off the old man, which is corrupt, and to put on the new man, which is created after God, in righteousness and true holiness! O what an unspeakable blessing is this! I almost stand amazed at the contemplation thereof. Well might the apostle exhort believers to rejoice in the Lord; indeed they have reason always to rejoice, yea, to rejoice on a dying bed; for the kingdom of God is in them; they are changed from glory to glory, even by the Spirit of the Lord: well may this be a mystery to the natural, for it is a mystery even to the spiritual man himself, a mystery which he cannot fathom. Does it not often dazzle your eyes, O ye children of God, to look at your own brightness, when the candle of the Lord shines out, and your Redeemer lifts up the light of his blessed countenance upon your souls? Are not you astonished, when you feel the love of God shed abroad in your hearts by the Holy Ghost, and God holds out the golden sceptre of his mercy, and bids you ask what you will, and it shall be given you? Does not that peace of God, which keeps and rules your hearts, surpass the utmost limits of your understandings? And is not the joy you feel unspeakable? Is it not full of glory? I am persuaded it is; and in your secret communion, when the Lord's love flows in upon your souls, you are as it were swallowed up in, or, to use the apostle's phrase, 'filled with all the fullness of God'. Are not you ready to cry out with Solomon, 'And will the Lord, indeed, dwell thus with men!' How is it that we should be thus thy sons and daughters, O Lord God Almighty!

If you are children of God, and know what it is to have

fellowship with the Father and the Son; if you walk by faith, and not by sight; I am assured this is frequently the language of your hearts.

But look forward, and see an unbounded prospect of eternal happiness lying before thee, O believer! what thou hast already received are only the first-fruits, like the cluster of grapes brought out of the land of Canaan; only an earnest and pledge of yet infinitely better things to come: the harvest is to follow; thy grace is hereafter to be swallowed up in glory. Thy great Joshua, and merciful High-Priest, shall administer an abundant entrance to thee into the land of promise, that rest which awaits the children of God: for Christ is not only made to believers wisdom, righteousness, and sanctification, but also *redemption*.

But, before we enter upon the explanation and contemplation of this privilege.

Firstly, Learn hence the great mistake of those writers and clergy, who, notwithstanding they talk of sanctification and inward holiness, (as indeed sometimes they do, though in a very loose and superficial manner,) yet they generally make it the *cause*, whereas they should consider it as the *effect*, of our justification. 'Of him are ye in Christ Jesus, who of God is made unto us, wisdom, righteousness, (and then) sanctification.' For Christ's righteousness, or that which Christ has done in our stead without us, is the sole cause of our acceptance in the sight of God, and of all holiness wrought in us: to this, and not to the light within, or any thing wrought within, should poor sinners seek for justification in the sight of God: for the sake of Christ's righteousness alone, and not any thing wrought in us, does God look favourably upon us; our sanctification at best, in this life, is not complete: though we be delivered from the power, we are not freed from the in-being of sin; but not only the dominion, but the in-being of sin, is forbidden, by the perfect law of God: for it is not said, thou shalt not give way to lust, but 'thou shalt not lust'. So that whilst the principle of lust remains in the least degree in our hearts, though we are otherwise never so holy, yet we cannot, on account of that, hope for acceptance with God. We must first, therefore, look for a righteousness without us, even the righteousness of our Lord Jesus Christ: for this reason the apostle mentions it, and puts it before sanctification, in the words of the text. And whosoever teacheth any other doctrine, doth not preach the truth as it is in Jesus.

Secondly, From hence also, the Antinomians and formal hypocrites may be confuted, who talk of Christ without, but know nothing, experimentally, of a work of sanctification wrought within them. Whatever they may pretend to, since Christ is not in them, the Lord is not their righteousness, and they have no well-grounded hope of glory: for though sanctification is not the cause, yet it is the effect of our acceptance with God; 'Who of God is made unto us righteousness and sanctification'. He, therefore, that is really in Christ, is a new creature; it is not going back to a covenant of works, to look into our hearts, and, seeing that they are changed and renewed, from thence form a comfortable and well grounded assurance of the safety of our states: no, but this is what we are directed to in scripture; by our bringing forth the fruits, we are to judge whether or no we ever did truly partake of the Spirit of God. 'We know (says John) that we are passed from death unto life, because we love the brethren.' And however we may talk of Christ's righteousness, and exclaim against legal preachers, yet, if we be not holy in heart and life, if we be not sanctified and renewed by the Spirit in our minds, we are self-deceivers, we are only formal hypocrites: for we must not put asunder what God has joined together; we must keep the medium between the two extremes; not insist so much on the one hand upon Christ without, as to exclude Christ within, as an evidence of our being his, and as a preparation for future happiness; nor, on the other hand, so depend on inherent righteousness or holiness wrought in us, as to exclude the righteousness of Jesus Christ without us. But,

4: *Fourthly*, Let us now go on, and take a view of the other link, or rather the end, of the believer's golden chain of privileges, *Redemption*. But we must look very high; for the top of it, like Jacob's ladder, reaches heaven, where all believers will ascend, and be placed at the right hand of God. 'Who of God is made unto us, wisdom, righteousness, sanctification, and *redemption*.'

This is a golden chain indeed! and, what is best of all, not one link can ever be broken asunder from another. Was there no other text in the book of God, this single one sufficiently proves the final perseverance of true believers: for never did God yet justify a man, whom he did not sanctify; nor sanctify one, whom he did not completely redeem and glorify: no! as for God, his way, his work, is perfect; he always carried on and finished the work he begun; thus it was in the first, so it is in the new creation; when God says, 'Let there be light', there is light, that shines more and more unto the perfect day, when believers enter into their eternal rest, as God entered into his. Those whom God has justified, he has in effect glorified: for as a man's worthiness was not the cause of God's giving him Christ's righteousness; so neither shall his unworthiness be a cause of his taking it away; God's gifts and callings are without repentance: and I cannot think they are clear in the notion of Christ's righteousness, who deny the final perseverance of the saints; I fear they understand justification in that low sense, which I understood it in a few years ago, as implying no more than remission of sins: but it not only signifies remission of sins past, but also a *federal right* to all good things to come. If God has given us his only Son, how shall he not with him freely give us all things? Therefore, the apostle, after he says, 'Who of God is made unto us righteousness', does not say, perhaps he may be made to us sanctification and redemption: but, 'he is made': for there is an eternal, indissoluble connexion between these blessed privileges. As the obedience of Christ is imputed to believers, so his perseverance in that obedience is to be imputed to them also; and it argues great ignorance of the covenant of grace and redemption, to object against it.

By the word *redemption*, we are to understand, not only a complete deliverance from all evil, but also a full enjoyment of all good both in body and soul: I say, both in body and soul; for the Lord is also for the body; the bodies of the saints in this life are temples of the Holy Ghost; God makes a covenant with the dust of believers; after death, though worms destroy them, yet, even in their flesh shall they see God. I fear, indeed, there are some Sadducees in our days, or at least heretics, who say, either, that there is no resurrection of the body, or that the resurrection is past already, namely, in our regeneration: Hence it is, that our Lord's coming in the flesh, at the day of judgment, is denied; and consequently, we must throw aside the sacrament of the Lord's supper. For why should we remember the Lord's death until he come to judgment, when he is already come to judge our hearts, and will not come a second time? But all this is only the reasoning of unlearned, unstable men, who certainly know not what they say, nor whereof they affirm. That we must follow our Lord in the regeneration, be partakers of a new birth, and that Christ must come into our hearts, we freely confess; and we hope, when speaking of these things, we speak no more than what we know and feel: but then it is plain, that Jesus Christ will come, hereafter, to judgment, and that he ascended into heaven with the body which he had here on earth; for says he, after his resurrection, 'Handle me, and see; a spirit has not flesh and bones, as you see me have'. And it is plain, that Christ's resurrection was an earnest of ours: for says the apostle, 'Christ is risen from the dead, and become the first-fruits of them that sleep; and as in Adam all die, and are subject to mortality; so all that are in Christ, the second Adam, who represented believers as their federal head, shall certainly be made alive, or rise again with their bodies at the last day'.

Here then, O believers! is one, though the lowest, degree of that redemption which you are to be partakers of hereafter; I mean, the redemption of your bodies: for this corruptible must put on incorruption, this mortal must put on immortality. Your bodies, as well as souls, were given to Jesus Christ by the Father; they have been companions in watching, and fasting, and praying: your bodies, therefore, as well as souls, shall Jesus Christ raise up at the last day. Fear not, therefore, O believers, to look into the grave: for to you it is no other than a consecrated dormitory, where your bodies shall sleep quietly until the morning of the resurrection; when the voice of the archangel shall sound, and the trump of God given the general alarm, 'Arise, ye dead, and come to judgment'; earth, air, fire, water, shall give up your scattered atoms, and both in body and soul shall you be ever with the Lord. I doubt not, but many of you are groaning under crazy bodies, and complain often that the mortal body weighs down the immortal soul; at least this is my case; but let us have a little patience, and we shall be delivered from our earthly prisons; ere long, these tabernacles of clay shall be dissolved, and we shall be clothed with our house which is from heaven; hereafter, our bodies shall be spiritualized, and shall be so far from hindering our souls through weakness, that they shall become strong; so strong, as to bear up under an exceeding and eternal weight of glory; others again may have deformed bodies, emaciated also with sickness, and worn out with labour and age; but wait a little, until your blessed change by death comes; then your bodies shall be renewed and made glorious, like unto Christ's glorious body: of which we may form some faint idea, from the account given us of our Lord's transfiguration on the mount, when it is said, 'His raiment became bright and glistening, and his face brighter than the sun'. Well then may a believer break out in the apostle's triumphant language, 'O death, where is thy sting! O grave, where is thy victory!'

But what is the redemption of the body, in comparison of the redemption of the better part, our souls? I must, therefore say to you believers, as the angel said to John, 'Come up higher'; and let us take as clear a view as we can, at such a distance, of the redemption Christ has purchased for, and will shortly put you in actual possession of. Already you are justified, already you are sanctified, and thereby freed from the guilt and dominion of sin: but, as I have observed, the being and indwelling of sin yet remains in you; God sees it proper to leave some Amalekites in the land, to keep his Israel in action. The most perfect Christian, I am persuaded, must agree, according to one of our Articles, 'That the corruption of nature remains even in the regenerate; that the flesh lusteth always against the spirit, and the spirit against the flesh'. So that believers cannot do things for God with that perfection they desire; this grieves their righteous souls day by day, and, with the holy apostle, makes them cry out, 'Who shall deliver us from the body of this death!' I thank God, our Lord Jesus Christ will, but not completely before the day of our dissolution; then will the very being of sin be destroyed, and an eternal stop put to inbred, indwelling corruption. And is not this a great redemption? I am sure believers esteem it so: for there is nothing grieves the heart of a child of God so much, as the remains of indwelling sin. Again, believers are often in heaviness through manifold temptations; God sees that it is needful and good for them so to be; and though they may be highly favoured, and wrapt up in communion with God, even to the third heavens; yet a messenger of Satan is often sent to buffet them, lest they should be puffed up with the abundance of revelations. But be not weary, be not faint in your minds: the time of your complete redemption draweth nigh. In heaven the wicked one shall cease from troubling you, and your weary souls shall enjoy an everlasting rest; his fiery darts cannot reach those blissful regions: Satan will never come any more to appear with, disturb, or accuse the sons of God, when once the Lord Jesus Christ shuts the door. Your righteous souls are now grieved, day by day, at the ungodly conversation of the wicked; tares now grow up among the wheat; wolves come in sheep's clothing: but the redemption spoken of in the text, will free your souls from all anxiety on these accounts; hereafter you shall enjoy a perfect communion of saints; nothing that is unholy or

unsanctified shall enter into the holy of holies, which is prepared for you above: this, and all manner of evil whatsoever, you shall be delivered from, when your redemption
is hereafter made complete in heaven; not only so, but you
shall enter into the full enjoyment of all good. It is true, all
saints will not have the same degree of happiness, but all
will be as happy as their hearts can desire. Believers, you
shall judge the evil, and familiarly converse with good,
angels: you shall sit down with Abraham, Isaac, Jacob, and
all the spirits of just men made perfect; and, to sum up all
your happiness in one word, you shall see God the Father,
Son, and Holy Ghost; and, by seeing God, be more and
more like unto him, and pass from glory to glory, even to
all eternity.

But I must stop: the glories of the upper world crowd in
so fast upon my soul, that I am lost in the contemplation of
them. Brethren, the redemption spoken of is unutterable; we
cannot here find it out; eye hath not seen, nor ear heard,
nor has it entered into the hearts of the most holy men
living to conceive, how great it is. Were I to entertain you
whole ages with an account of it, when you come to heaven,
you must say, with the queen of Sheba, 'Not half, no, not
one thousandth part was told us'. All we can do here, is to go
upon mount Pisgah, and, by the eye of faith, take a distant
view of the promised land: we may see it, as Abraham did
Christ, afar off, and rejoice in it; but here we only know in
part. Blessed be God, there is a time coming, when we shall
know God, even as we are known, and God be all in all. Lord
Jesus, accomplish the number of thine elect! Lord Jesus,
hasten thy kingdom!

And now, where are the scoffers of these last days, who
count the lives of Christians to be madness, and their end to

be without honour? Unhappy men! you know not what you do. Were your eyes open, and had you senses to discern spiritual things, you would not speak all manner of evil against the children of God, but you would esteem them as the excellent ones of the earth, and envy their happiness: your souls would hunger and thirst after it: you also would become fools for Christ's sake. You boast of wisdom; so did the philosophers of Corinth: but your wisdom is the foolishness of folly in the sight of God. What will your wisdom avail you, if it does not make you wise unto salvation? Can you, with all your wisdom, propose a more consistent scheme to build you hopes of salvation on, than what has been now laid before you? Can you, with all the strength of natural reason, find out a better way of acceptance with God, than by the righteousness of the Lord Jesus Christ? Is it right to think your own works can in any measure deserve or procure it? If not, why will you not believe in him? Why will you not submit to his righteousness? Can you deny that you are fallen creatures? Do not you find that you are full of disorders, and that these disorders make you unhappy? Do not you find that you cannot change your own hearts? Have you not resolved many and many a time, and have not your corruptions yet dominion over you? Are you not bondslaves to your lusts, and led captive by the devil at his will? Why then will you not come to Christ for sanctification? Do you not desire to die the death of the righteous, and that your future state may be like theirs; I am persuaded you cannot bear the thoughts of being annihilated, much less of being miserable for ever. Whatever you may pretend, if you speak truth, you must confess, that conscience breaks in upon you in more sober intervals whether you will or not, and even constrains you to believe that hell is no painted fire. And why then will you not come to Christ? He alone can procure you everlasting redemption. Haste, haste away to him, poor beguiled sinners. You lack wisdom; ask it of Christ. Who knows but he may give it you? He is able: for he is the wisdom of the Father; he is that wisdom which was from everlasting. You have no righteousness; away, therefore, to Christ: 'He is the end of the law for righteousness to every one that believeth.' You are unholy: flee to the Lord Jesus: He is full of grace and truth; and of his fullness all may receive that believe in him. You are afraid to die; let this drive you to Christ: he has the keys of death and hell: in him is plenteous redemption; he alone can open the door which leads to everlasting life.

Let not, therefore, the deceived reasoner boast any longer of his pretended reason. Whatever you may think, it is the most unreasonable thing in the world not to believe on Jesus Christ, whom God has sent. Why, why will you die? Why will you not come unto him, that you may have life? 'Ho! every one that thirsteth, come unto the waters of life, and drink freely: come, buy without money and without price.' Were these blessed privileges in the text to be purchased with money, you might say, we are poor, and cannot buy: or, were they to be conferred only on sinners of such a rank or degree, then you might say, how can such sinners as we, expect to be so highly favoured? But they are to be freely given of God to the worst of sinners. 'To us', says the apostle, to me a persecutor, to you Corinthians, who were 'unclean, drunkards, covetous persons, idolators.' Therefore, each poor sinner may say then, why not unto me? Has Christ but one blessing? What if he has blessed millions already, by turning them away from their iniquities; yet he still continues the same: he lives for ever to make intercession, and therefore will bless you, even you also. Though, Esau-like, you have been profane, and hitherto despised your heavenly Father's birth-right; even now, if you believe, 'Christ will be made to you of God, wisdom, righteousness, sanctification, and redemption'.

But I must turn again to believers, for whose instruction, as I observed before, this discourse was particularly intended. You see, brethren, partakers of the heavenly calling, what great blessings are treasured up for you in Jesus Christ your Head, and what you are entitled to by believing on his name. Take heed, therefore, that ye walk worthy of the vocation wherewith ye are called. Think often how highly you are favoured; and remember, you have not chosen Christ, but Christ has chosen you. Put on (as the elect of God) humbleness of mind, and glory, but let it be only in the Lord; for you have nothing but what you have received of God. By nature ye were foolish, as legal, as unholy, and in as damnable a condition, as others. Be pitiful, therefore, be courteous; and, as sanctification is a progressive work, beware of thinking you have already attained. Let him that is holy be holy still; knowing, that he who is most pure in heart, shall hereafter enjoy the clearest vision of God. Let indwelling sin be your daily burden; and not only bewail and lament, but see that you subdue it daily by the power of divine grace; and look up to Jesus continually to be the finisher, as well as author, of your faith. Build not on your own faithfulness, but on God's unchangeableness. Take heed of thinking you stand by the power of your own free will. The everlasting love of God the Father, must be your only hope and consolation; let this support you under all trials. Remember that God's gifts and callings are without repentance; that Christ having once loved you, will love you to the end. Let this constrain you to obedience, and make you long and look for that blessed time, when he shall not only be your wisdom, and righteousness, and sanctification, but also complete and everlasting redemption.

Glory be to God in the highest!

THE LORD OUR RIGHTEOUSNESS

The Lord our Righteousness. *Jer* 23.6

Whoever is acquainted with the nature of mankind in general, or the propensity of his own heart in particular, must acknowledge, that *self-righteousness* is the last idol that is rooted out of the heart: being once born under a covenant of works, it is natural for us all to have recourse to a covenant of works for our everlasting salvation. And we have contracted such a devilish pride by our fall from God, that we would, if not wholly, yet in part at least, glory in being the cause of our own salvation. We cry out against popery, and that very justly; but we are all Papists; at least, I am sure, we are all Arminians by nature; and, therefore, no wonder so many natural men embrace that scheme. It is true, we disclaim the doctrine of merit, are ashamed directly to say we deserve any good at the hands of God; therefore, as the apostle excellently well observes, 'we go about', we fetch a circuit, 'to establish a righteousness of our own, and', like the Pharisees of old, 'will not wholly submit to that righteousness which is of God through Jesus Christ our Lord'.

This is the sorest, though, alas! the most common evil that was ever yet seen under the sun. An evil, that in any age, especially in these dregs of time wherein we live, cannot sufficiently be inveighed against. For as it is with the people, so it is with the priests; and it is to be feared, even in those places, where once the truth, as it is in Jesus, was eminently preached, many ministers, are so sadly degenerated from their pious ancestors, that the doctrines of grace, especially the personal, *all-sufficient righteousness of Jesus*, is but too seldom, too slightly mentioned. Hence the love of many waxeth cold; and I have often thought, were it possible, that this single consideration would be sufficient to raise our venerable forefathers again from their graves; who would thunder in their ears their fatal error.

The righteousness of Jesus Christ is one of those great mysteries which the angels desire to look into, and seems to be one of the first lessons that God taught men after the fall. For, what were the coats that God made to put on our first parents, but types of the application of the merits or righteousness of Jesus Christ to believers' hearts? We are told, that those coats were made of skins of beasts; and, as beasts were not then food for men, we may fairly infer, that those beasts were slain in sacrifice, in commemoration of the great sacrifice, Jesus Christ, thereafter to be offered. And the skins of the beasts thus slain, being put on Adam and Eve, they were hereby taught how their nakedness was to be covered with the righteousness of the Lamb of God.

This is it which is meant, when we are told, 'Abraham believed on the Lord, and it was accounted to him for righteousness'. In short, this is it of which both the law and the prophets have spoken, especially Jeremiah in the words of the text, 'The Lord our righteousness'.

I propose, through divine grace,

1: To consider whom we are to understand by the word Lord.

ii: How the Lord is man's righteousness.

iii: I will consider some of the chief objections that are generally urged against this doctrine.

iv: I shall shew some very ill consequences that flow naturally from denying this doctrine.

v: Shall conclude with an exhortation to all to come to Christ by faith, that they may be enabled to say with the prophet in the text, 'The Lord our righteousness'.

i: I am to consider whom we are to understand by the word Lord: The Lord our righteousness.

If any Arians or Socinians are drawn by curiosity to hear what the babbler has to say, let them be ashamed of denying the divinity of that Lord, who has bought poor sinners with his precious blood. For the person mentioned in the text, under the character of the Lord, is Jesus Christ. Verse 5. 'Behold, the days come, saith the Lord, that I will raise unto David a righteous branch, a king shall reign and prosper, and shall execute judgment and justice in the earth. In his days (ver. 6) Judah shall be saved, and Israel shall dwell safely; and this is his name whereby he shall be called, The Lord our righteousness.' By the *righteous branch*, all agree that we are to understand Jesus Christ. He it is that is called the Lord in our text. If so, if there were no other text in the Bible to prove the divinity of Christ, this is sufficient: for if the word *Lord* may properly belong to Jesus Christ, he must be God. And, as you have it in the margin of your Bibles, the word *Lord* is, in the original, *Jehovah*, which is the essential title of God himself. Come then, ye Arians, kiss the Son of God, bow down before him, and honour him, even as ye honour the Father. Learn of the angels, those morning-stars, and worship him as truly God: for otherwise you are as much idolaters as those that worship the virgin

Mary. And as for you Socinians, who say Christ was a mere man, and yet profess that he was your Saviour; according to your own principles you are accursed: for, if Christ be a mere man, then he is only an arm of flesh: and it is written, 'Cursed is he that trusteth on an arm of flesh'. But I would hope there are no such monsters here; at least, that, after these considerations, they would be ashamed of broaching such monstrous absurdities any more. For it is plain, that, by the word *Lord*, we are to understand the Lord Jesus Christ, who here takes to himself the title of *Jehovah*, and therefore must be very God of very God; or, as the apostle devoutly expresses it, 'God blessed for evermore'.

II. How the Lord is to be man's righteousness, comes next to be considered.

And that is, in one word, by *imputation*. For it pleased God, after he had made all things by the word of his power, to create man after his own image. And so infinite was the condescension of the high and lofty One who inhabiteth eternity, that although he might have insisted on the everlasting obedience of him and his posterity; yet he was pleased to oblige himself, by a covenant, or agreement, made with his own creatures, upon condition of an unsinning obedience, to give them immortality and eternal life. For when it is said, 'The day thou eatest thereof, thou shalt surely die': we may fairly infer, so long as he continued obedient, and did not eat thereof, he should surely live. The 3rd of Genesis gives us a full, but mournful account, how our first parents broke this covenant, and thereby stood in need of a better righteousness than their own, in order to procure their future acceptance with God. For what must they do? They were as much under a covenant of works as ever. And though, after their disobedience, they were without strength, yet they were obliged not only to do, but to continue to do all things, and that too in the most perfect manner, which the Lord had required of them: and not only so, but to make satisfaction to God's infinitely offended justice for the breach they had already been guilty of. Here then opens the amazing scene of *divine philanthropy*; I mean, God's love to man: for, behold, what man could not do, Jesus Christ, the Son of his Father's love, undertakes to do for him. And that God might be just in justifying the ungodly, though 'he was in the form of God, and therefore thought it no robbery to be equal with God; yet he took upon him the form of a servant', even human nature. In that nature he obeyed, and thereby fulfilled the whole moral law in our stead: and also died a painful death upon the cross, and thereby became a curse for, or instead of, those whom the Father had given to him. As God, he satisfied, at the same time that he obeyed and suffered as man; and being God and man in one person, he wrought out a full, perfect, and sufficient righteousness for all to whom it was to be imputed.

Here then we see the meaning of the word *righteousness*. It implies the active as well as passive obedience of the Lord Jesus Christ. We generally, when talking of the merits of Christ, only mention the latter, his death; whereas the former, his life and active obedience, is equally necessary. Christ is not such a Saviour as becomes us, unless we join both together. Christ not only died, but lived; not only suffered, but obeyed for, or instead of, poor sinners. And both these jointly make up that complete righteousness which is to be imputed to us, as the disobedience of our first parents was made ours by imputation. In this sense, and no other, are we to understand that parallel which the apostle

Paul draws in the fifth of the Romans, between the first and second Adam. This is what he elsewhere terms, 'our being made the righteousness of God in him'. This is the sense wherein the prophet would have us to understand the words of the text; therefore, Jer 33.16: 'She (that is, the church itself) shall be called, (having this righteousness imputed to her,) the Lord our righteousness': a passage, I think, worthy of the profoundest meditation of all the sons and daughters of Abraham.

Many are the objections which the proud hearts of fallen men are continually urging against this wholesome, this divine, this soul-saving doctrine. I come now,

III: To answer some few of those which I think the most considerable.

And, *First*, They say, because they would appear friends to morality, 'That the doctrine of an imputed righteousness is destructive of good works, and leads to licentiousness'.

And who, pray, are the persons that generally urge this objection? Are they men full of faith, and men really concerned for good works? No; whatever few exceptions there may be, if there be any at all, it is notorious they are generally men of corrupt minds, reprobate concerning the faith. The best title I can give them is, that of *profane moralists*, or moralists falsely so called. For I appeal to the experience of the present, as well as past ages, if iniquity did and does not most abound, where the doctrine of Christ's whole personal righteousness is most cried down, and most seldom mentioned: Arminian, being antichristian, principles, always did, and always will, lead to antichristian practices. And never was there a reformation brought about in the church, but by preaching the doctrine of an imputed righteousness. This, as that man of God, Luther, calls it, is *articulis stantis aut cadentis ecclesiæ*, the article by which the church stands or falls. And though the preachers of this doctrine are generally branded, by those on the other side, with the opprobrious names of Antinomians, deceivers, and what not, yet, I believe, if the truth of the doctrine, on both sides, was to be judged of by the lives of the preachers and professors of it, on our side the question would have the advantage every way.

It is true, this, as well as every other doctrine of grace, may be abused. And perhaps the unchristian walk of some, who have talked of Christ's imputed righteousness, justification by faith, and the like, and yet never felt it imputed to their own souls, has given the enemies of the Lord thus cause to blaspheme. But this is a very unsafe, as well as a very unfair, way of arguing. The only question should be, whether or not this doctrine of an imputed righteousness does in itself cut off the occasion of good works, or lead to licentiousness? To this we may boldly answer, In no wise. It excludes works, indeed, from being any cause of our justification in the sight of God; but it requires good works as a proof of our having this righteousness imputed to us, and as a declarative evidence of our justification in the sight of men. And then, how can the doctrine of an imputed righteousness be a doctrine leading to licentiousness?

It is all calumny. The apostle Paul introduceth an infidel making this objection in his epistle to the Romans; and none but infidels, that never felt the power of Christ's resurrection upon their souls, will urge it over again. And therefore, notwithstanding this objection, with the prophet of the text we may boldly say, 'The Lord is our righteousness'.

But Satan (and no wonder that his servants imitate him) often transforms him into an angel of light; and therefore, (such perverse things will infidelity and Arminianism make men speak) in order to dress their objections in the best colours, some urge, 'That our Saviour preached no such doctrine; that in his sermon on the mount, he mentions only morality; and consequently the doctrine of an imputed righteousness falls wholly to the ground'.

But surely the men who urge this objection, either never read, or never understood, our Lord's blessed discourse, wherein the doctrine of an imputed righteousness is so plainly taught, that he who runs, if he have eyes that see, may read.

Indeed, our Lord does recommend morality and good works, (as all faithful ministers will do,) and clears the moral law from many corrupt glosses put upon it by the letter-learned Pharisees. But then, before he comes to this, it is remarkable, he talks of inward piety, such as poverty of spirit, meekness, holy mourning, purity of heart, especially hungering and thirsting after righteousness; and then recommends good works, as an evidence of our having his righteousness imputed to us, and these graces and divine tempers wrought in our hearts. 'Let your light (that is, the divine light I before have been mentioning) shine before men in a holy life; that they, seeing your good works, may glorify your Father which is in heaven.' And then he immediately adds, 'Think not that I am come to destroy the moral law: I came not to destroy, (to take away the force of it as a rule of life,) but to fulfil, (to obey it in its whole latitude, and give the complete sense of it)'. And then he goes on to shew how exceedingly broad the moral law is. So that our Lord, instead of setting aside an imputed righteousness, in his sermon upon the mount, not only confirms it, but also answers the foregoing objection urged against it, by making good works a proof and evidence of its being imputed to our souls. He, therefore, that hath ears to hear, let him hear what the prophet says in the words of the text, 'The Lord our righteousness'.

But as Satan not only quoted scripture, but backed one temptation after another with it, when he attacked Christ in the wilderness; so his children generally take the same method in treating his doctrine. And, therefore, they urge another objection against the doctrine of an imputed righteousness, from the example of the young man in the gospel.

We may state it thus: 'The evangelist Mark, say they, Chap. 10, mentions a young man that came to Christ, running, and asking what he should do to inherit eternal life? Christ referred him to the commandments, to know what he must do to inherit eternal life. It is plain, therefore, works were to be, partly at least, the cause of his justification: and consequently the doctrine of an imputed righteousness is unscriptural'. This is the objection in its full strength: and little strength in all its fullness, For, were I to prove the necessity of an imputed righteousness, I scarce know how I could bring a better instance to make it good.

Let us take a nearer view of this young man, and of our Lord's behaviour towards him: Mark 10.17. The evangelist tells us, 'That when Christ was gone forth into the way, there came one running, (it should seem it was some nobleman, a rarity indeed to see such a one running to Christ!) and not only so, but he kneeled to him, (perhaps many of his rank now scarce know the time when they kneeled to Christ,) and asked him, saying, "Good Master, what shall I do, that I may inherit eternal life?" Then Jesus, to see whether or not he believed him to be what he really was, truly and properly

God, said unto him, "Why callest thou me good? There is none good but one, that is, God". And that he might directly answer his question, says he, "Thou knowest the commandments: do not commit adultery, do not bear false witness, defraud not, honour thy father and thy mother".' This was a direct answer to his question; namely, That eternal life was not to be attained by his doings. For our Lord by referring him to the commandments, did not, as the objectors insinuate, in the least hint that his morality would recommend him to the favour and mercy of God: but he intended thereby, to make the law his schoolmaster to bring him to himself; that the young man, seeing how he had broken everyone of these commandments, might thereby be convinced of the insufficiency of his own, and consequently of the absolute necessity of looking out for a better righteousness, whereon he might depend for eternal life.

This was what our Lord designed. The young man being self-righteous, and willing to justify himself, said, 'All these have I observed from my youth'; but had he known himself, he would have confessed, all these have I broken from my youth. For, supposing he never actually committed adultery, had he never lusted after a woman in his heart? What if he had not really killed another, had he never been angry without a cause, or spoken unadvisedly with his lips? If so, by breaking one of the least commandments in the least degree, he became liable to the curse of God; for "cursed is he (saith the law) that continueth not to do all things that are written in this book." And therefore, as observed before, our Lord was so far from speaking against, that he treated the young man in that manner, on purpose to convince him of the necessity of an imputed righteousness.

But, perhaps, they will reply, it is said, 'Jesus beholding him, loved him.' And what then? This he might do with a human love, and at the same time this young man have no interest in his blood. Thus Christ is said to wonder, to weep over Jerusalem, and say, "O that thou hadst known," etc. But such-like passages are to be referred only to his human nature. And there is a great deal of difference between the love wherewith Christ loved this young man, and that wherewith he loved Mary, Lazarus, and their sister Martha. To illustrate this by a comparison: a minister of the Lord Jesus Christ, seeing many amiable dispositions, such as a readiness to hear the word, a decent behaviour at public worship, and a life outwardly spotless in many, cannot but so far love them; but then, there is much difference betwixt the love which a minister feels for such, and that divine love, that union and sympathy of soul, which he feels for those that he is satisfied are really born again of God. Apply this to our Lord's case, as a faint illustration of it. Consider what has been said upon the young man's case in general, and then, if before you were fond of this objection, instead of triumphing, like him you will go sorrowful away. Our Saviour's reply to him, more and more convinces us of the truth of the prophet's assertion in the text, that 'the Lord is our righteousness.'

But there is a fourth, and a grand objection yet behind, which is taken from the 25th chapter of Matthew, 'where our Lord is described as rewarding people with eternal life, because they fed the hungry, clothed the naked, and such like. Their works, therefore, were a cause of their justification, consequently the doctrine of imputed righteousness is not agreeable to scripture'.

This, I confess, is the most plausible objection that is

brought against the doctrine insisted on from the text; and that we may answer it in as clear and brief a manner as may be, we confess, with the article of the Church of England, 'That albeit good works do not justify us, yet they will follow after justification, as fruits of it; and though they can claim no reward in themselves, yet forasmuch as they spring from faith in Christ, and a renewed soul, they shall receive a reward of grace, though not of debt; and consequently, the more we abound in such good works, the greater will be our reward when Jesus Christ shall come to judgment'.

Take these considerations along with us, and they will help us much to answer the objection now before us. For thus saith Matthew, 'Then shall the King say to them on his right hand, Come, ye blessed children of my Father, inherit the kingdom prepared for you from the foundation of the world. For I was an hungred, and ye gave me meat; I was thirsty, and ye gave me drink; I was a stranger, and ye took me in; naked, and ye clothed me; I was sick, and ye visited me; I was in prison, and ye came unto me. I will therefore reward you, because you have done these things out of love to me, and hereby have evidenced yourselves to be my true disciples.' And that the people did not depend on these good actions for their justification in the sight of God, is evident: 'For when saw we thee an hungred, (they say), and fed thee? or thirsty, and gave thee drink? When saw we thee a stranger, and took thee in; or naked, and clothed thee? Or when saw we thee sick, or in prison, and came unto thee?' Language, and questions, quite improper for persons relying on their own righteousness for acceptance and acquittance in the sight of God.

But then they reply against this: 'In the latter part of the chapter, it is plain that Jesus Christ rejects and damns the others for not doing these things. And therefore, if he damn these for not doing, he saves those for doing; and consequently the doctrine of an imputed righteousness is good for nothing.'

But that is no consequence at all; for God may justly damn any man for omitting the least duty of the moral law, and yet in himself is not obliged to give to any one any reward, supposing he has done all that he can. We are unprofitable servants, we have not done near so much as it was our duty to do, — must be the language of the most holy souls living; and therefore, from, or in ourselves, we cannot be justified in the sight of God. This was the frame of the devout souls just now referred to. Sensible of this, they were so far from depending on their works for justification in the sight of God, that they were filled, as it were, with a holy blushing, to think our Lord should condescend to mention, much more to reward them for, their poor works of faith and labours of love. I am persuaded their hearts would rise with a holy indignation against those who urge this passage as an objection to the assertion of the prophet, that 'the Lord is our righteousness'.

Thus, I think, we have fairly answered these grand objections, which are generally urged against the doctrine of an *imputed righteousness*. Was I to stop here, I think I may say, 'We are made more than conquerors through him that loved us.' But there is a way of arguing which I have always admired, because I have thought it always very convincing, by shewing the *absurdities* that will follow from denying any particular proposition in dispute.

IV: This is the next thing that was proposed. And never did greater or more absurdities flow from the denying any doctrine, than will flow from denying the doctrine of Christ's imputed righteousness.

And *first*, If we deny this doctrine, we turn the truth, I mean the word of God, as much as we can, into a lie, and utterly subvert all those places of scripture which say that we are saved by grace; that it is not of works, lest any man should boast; that salvation is God's free gift; and that he who glorieth must glory only in the Lord. For, if the whole personal righteousness of Jesus Christ be not the sole cause of my acceptance with God, if any work done by or foreseen in me, was in the least to be joined with it, or looked upon by God as an inducing, impulsive cause of acquitting my soul from guilt, then I have somewhat whereof I may glory in myself. Now, boasting is excluded in the great work of our redemption; but that cannot be, if we are enemies to the doctrine of an imputed righteousness. It would be endless to enumerate how many texts of scripture must be false, if this doctrine be not true. Let it suffice to affirm in the general, that if we deny an imputed righteousness, we may as well deny a divine revelation all at once: for it is the *alpha* and *omega*, the beginning and the end, of the book of God. We must either disbelieve that, or believe what the prophet hath spoken in the text, that "the Lord is our righteousness."

But further: I observed at the beginning of this discourse, that we were all Arminians and Papists by nature; for, as one says, 'Arminianism is the back way to popery'. And here I venture further to affirm, that if we deny the doctrine of an imputed righteousness, whatever we may style ourselves, we are really Papists in our hearts, and deserve no other title from men.

Sirs, what think you? Suppose I were to come and tell

you, that you must intercede with saints, for them to intercede with God for you; would you not then say, I was justly reputed a popish missionary by some, and deservedly thrust out of the synagogues by others? I suppose you would. And why? Because, you would say, the intercession of Jesus Christ was sufficient of itself, without the intercession of saints; and that it was blasphemous to join theirs with his, as though it was not sufficient.

Suppose I went a little more round about, and told you that the death of Christ was not sufficient, without our death being added to it; that you must die as well as Christ, join your death with his, and then it would be sufficient. Might you not then, with a holy indignation, throw dust in the air, and justly call me a 'setter forth of strange doctrines?' And now then, if it be not only absurd, but blasphemous, to join the intercession of saints with the intercession of Christ, as though his intercession was not sufficient; or our death with the death of Christ, as though his death was not sufficient: judge ye, if it be not equally absurd, equally blasphemous, to join our obedience, either wholly or in part, with the obedience of Christ, as if that were not sufficient. And if so, what absurdities will follow the denying that the Lord, both as to his active and passive obedience, is our righteousness!

One more absurdity I shall mention, as following the denying this doctrine, and I have done.

I remember a story of a certain prelate, who after many arguments, in vain urged to convince the earl of Rochester of the invisible realities of another world, took his leave of his lordship with some such words as these: 'Well, my lord, if there be no hell, I am safe: but if there should be such a thing as hell, what will become of you?' I apply this to those that oppose the doctrine now insisted on. If there be no such thing as the doctrine of an imputed righteousness, those who hold it, and bring forth fruit unto holiness, are safe: but if there be such a thing (as there certainly is) what will become of you that deny it? It is no difficult matter to determine. Your portion must be in the lake of fire and brimstone for ever and ever. Since you will rely upon your works, by your works you shall be judged. They shall be weighed in the balance of the sanctuary; and they will be found wanting. By your works, therefore, shall you be condemned! and you, being out of Christ, shall find God, to your poor wretched souls, a consuming fire.

The great Stoddard of Northampton, in New England, has therefore, well entitled a book which he wrote, (and which I would take this opportunity to recommend,) 'The Safety of appearing at the Day of Judgement in the Righteousness of Christ'. For why should I lean upon a broken reed, when I can have the Rock of ages to stand upon, that never can be moved?

And now, before I come to a more particular application, give me leave, in the apostle's language, triumphantly to cry out, 'Where is the scribe, where is the disputer?' Where is the reasoning infidel of this generation? Can any thing appear more reasonable, even according to your own way of arguing, than the doctrine here laid down? Have you not felt a convincing power go along with the Word? Why then will you not believe on the Lord Jesus Christ, that so he may become the Lord *your* righteousness.

But it is time for me to come a little closer to your consciences.

Brethren, though some may be offended at this doctrine, and may account it foolishness, yet, to many of you, I doubt not but it is precious, it being agreeable to the form of sound words, which from your infancy has been delivered to you; and, coming from a quarter you would least have expected, may be received with more pleasure and satisfaction. But give me leave to ask you one question: Can you say, the Lord our righteousness? I say, the Lord *our* righteousness. For entertaining this doctrine in your heads, without receiving the Lord Jesus Christ savingly by a lively faith into your hearts, will but increase your damnation. As I have often told you, so I tell you again, — an unapplied Christ is no Christ at all. Can you then, with believing Thomas, cry out, 'My Lord and my God?' Is Christ your sanctification, as well as your outward righteousness? For the word righteousness, in the text, not only implies Christ's personal righteousness imputed to us, but also holiness wrought in us. These two, God has joined together. He never did, he never does, he never will, put them asunder. If you are justified by the blood, you are also sanctified by the Spirit, of our Lord. Can you then in this sense say, The Lord our righteousness? Were you ever made to abhor yourselves for your actual and original sins, and to loathe your own righteousness; for, as the prophet beautifully expresses it, 'your righteousness is as filthy rags?' Were you ever made to see and admire the all-sufficiency of Christ's righteousness, and excited by the Spirit of God to hunger and thirst after it? Could you ever say, My soul is athirst for Christ, yea, even for the righteousness of Christ? O when shall I come to appear before the presence of my God in the righteousness of Christ! nothing but Christ! nothing but Christ! Give me Christ, O God, and I am satisfied! my soul shall praise thee for ever.

Was this ever the language of your hearts? and, after

these inward conflicts, were you ever enabled to reach out the arm of faith, and embrace the blessed Jesus in your souls, so that you could say, 'My Beloved is mine, and I am his?' If so, fear not, whoever you are. Hail, all hail, you happy souls! The Lord, the Lord Christ, the everlasting God, is your righteousness. Christ has justified you, who is he that condemneth you? Christ has died for you, nay, rather, is risen again, and ever liveth to make intercession for you. Being now justified by his grace, you have peace with God, and shall, ere long, be with Jesus in glory, reaping everlasting and unspeakable fruits both in body and soul. For there is no condemnation to those that are really in Christ Jesus. Whether Paul, or Apollos, or life, or death, all is yours, if you are Christ's, for Christ is God's. My brethren, my heart is enlarged towards you! O think of the love of Christ in dying for you! If the Lord be your righteousness, let the righteousness of your Lord be continually in your mouth. Talk of, O talk of, and recommend the righteousness of Christ, when you lie down, and when you rise up, at your going out and coming in! Think of the greatness of the gift, as well as of the giver! Shew to all the world, in whom you have believed! Let all by your fruits know, that the Lord is your righteousness, and that you are waiting for your Lord from heaven! O study to be holy, even as he who has called you, and washed you in his own blood, is holy! Let not the righteousness of the Lord be evil spoken of through you. Let not Jesus be wounded in the house of his friends; but grow in grace, and in the knowledge of our Lord and Saviour Jesus Christ, day by day. O think of his dying love! Let that love constrain you to obedience! Having much forgiven, love much. Be always asking, What shall I do to express my gratitude to the Lord for giving me his righteousness? Let that self-abasing, God-exalting question, be always in your mouths: 'Why me, Lord? why me?' why am I taken, and others left? why is the Lord my righteousness? why is he become my salvation, who have so often deserved damnation at his hands?

My friends, I trust I feel somewhat of a sense of God's distinguishing love upon my heart; therefore I must divert a little from congratulating you, to invite poor christless sinners to come to him, and accept of his righteousness, that they may have life.

Alas, my heart almost bleeds! What a multitude of precious souls are now before me! how shortly must all be ushered into eternity! and yet, O cutting thought! were God now to require all your souls, how few, comparatively speaking, could really say, the Lord *our* righteousness!

And think you, *O sinners*, that you will be able to stand in the day of judgment, if Christ be not your righteousness! No, that alone is the wedding-garment in which you must appear. O Christless sinners, I am distressed for you! the desires of my soul are enlarged. O that this may be an accepted time! that the Lord may be your righteousness! For whither would you flee, if death should find you naked? Indeed, there is no hiding yourselves from his presence. The pitiful fig-leaves of your own righteousness will not cover your nakedness, when God shall call you to stand before him. Adam found them ineffectual, and so will you. O think of death! O think of judgment! Yet a little while, and time shall be no more; and then what will become of you, if the Lord be not your righteousness? Think you that Christ will spare you? No, he that formed you, will have no mercy on you. If you be not of Christ, if Christ be not your righteousness, Christ himself shall pronounce you damned. And can

ness or number of your sins. For are you sinners? so am I. Are you the chief of sinners? so am I. Are you backsliding sinners? so am I. And yet the Lord (for ever adored be his rich, free, and sovereign grace!), the Lord is my righteousness. Come, then, *O young men*, who (as I acted once myself) are playing the prodigal, and wandering away afar off from your heavenly Father's house, come home, come home, and leave your swine's trough. Feed no longer on the husks of sensual delights: for Christ's sake arise, and come home! your heavenly Father now calls you. See yonder the best robe, even the righteousness of his dear Son, awaits you. See it, view it again and again. Consider at how dear a rate it was purchased, even by the blood of God. Consider what great need you have of it. You are lost, undone, damned for ever, without it. Come then, poor, guilty prodigals, come home; indeed, I will not, like the elder brother in the Gospel, be angry; no, I will rejoice with the angels in heaven. And O that God would now bow the heavens and come down! Descend, O Son of God, descend; and, as thou hast shewn in me such mercy, O let thy blessed Spirit apply thy righteousness to some young prodigals now before thee, and clothe their naked souls with thy best robe!

But I must speak a word to you, *young maidens*, as well as young men. I see many of you adorned, as to your bodies: but are not your souls naked? Which of you can say, the Lord is my righteousness? which of you was ever solicitous to be dressed in this robe of invaluable price, and without which you are no better than whited sepulchres in the sight of God? Let not then so many of you, young maidens, any longer forget your chief and only ornament. O seek for the Lord to be your righteousness, or otherwise burning will soon be upon you instead of beauty!

And what shall I say to you of a middle age, you *busy merchants*, you *cumbered Marthas*, who, with all your gettings, have not yet gotten the Lord to be your righteousness? Alas! what profit will there be of all your labour under the sun, if you do not secure this pearl of invaluable price? this one thing so absolutely needful, that it only can stand you in stead, when all other things shall be taken from you. Labour therefore, no longer, so anxiously for the meat which perisheth, but henceforward seek for the Lord to be your righteousness, a righteousness that will entitle you to life everlasting. I see, also, many *hoary heads* here, and perhaps the most of them cannot say, the Lord is my righteousness. O grey-headed sinners, I could weep over you! your grey hairs, which ought to be your crown, and in which perhaps you glory, are now your shame. You know not that the Lord is your righteousness: O haste then, haste ye, aged sinners, and seek an interest in redeeming love! Alas, you have one foot already in the grave, your glass is just run out, your sun is just going down, and it will set and leave you in an eternal darkness, unless the Lord be your righteousness! Flee then, O flee for your lives! be not afraid. All things are possible with God. If you come, though it be at the eleventh hour, Christ Jesus will in no wise cast you out. Seek then for the Lord to be your righteousness, and beseech him to let you know how it is that a man may be born again when he is old! But I must not forget the *lambs* of the flock. To feed them was one of my Lord's last commands. I know he will be angry with me, if I do not tell them that the Lord may be *their* righteousness, and that of such is the kingdom of heaven. Come then, ye little children, come to Christ; the Lord Christ shall be *your* righteousness. Do not think that you are too young to be converted. Perhaps many of you may be nine or ten years old, and yet cannot say, the Lord is our righteousness; which many have said, though younger than you. Come, then, while you are young. Perhaps you may not live to be old. Do not stay for other people. If your fathers and mothers will not come to Christ, do you come without them. Let children lead them, and shew them how the Lord may be *their* righteousness. Our Lord Jesus loved little children. You are his lambs; he bids me feed you. I pray God make you willing betimes to take the Lord for your righteousness.

Here, then, I could conclude; but I must not forget the *poor negroes*: no, I must not. Jesus Christ has died for them, as well as for others. Nor do I mention you last, because I despise your souls, but because I would have what I shall say make the deeper impression upon your hearts. O that you would seek the Lord to be your righteousness! Who knows but he may be found of you? For in Jesus Christ there is neither male nor female, bond nor free; even you may be the children of God, if you believe in Jesus. Did you never read of the eunuch belonging to the queen Candace? a negro, like yourselves. He believed. The Lord was his righteousness. He was baptized. Do you also believe, and you shall be saved. Christ Jesus is the same now as he was yesterday, and will wash you in his own blood. Go home then, turn the words of the text into a prayer, and entreat the Lord to be *your* righteousness. Even so, come, Lord Jesus, come quickly into all our souls; *Amen*. Lord Jesus, *amen*, and *amen*!

THE SEED OF THE WOMAN AND THE
SEED OF THE SERPENT

And I will put enmity between thee and the
woman, and between thy seed and her seed; it shall
bruise thy head, and thou shalt bruise his heel.
Gen 3.15

On reading to you these words, I may address you in the
language of the holy angels to the shepherds, that were
watching their flocks by night; 'Behold, I bring you glad
tidings of great joy'. For this is the first promise that was
made of a Saviour to the apostate race of Adam. We
generally look for Christ only in the New Testament; but
Christianity, in one sense, is very near as old as the creation.
It is wonderful to observe how gradually God revealed his
Son to mankind. He began with the promise in the text,
and this the elect lived upon till the time of Abraham. To
him, God made further discoveries of his eternal counsel
concerning man's redemption. Afterwards, at sundry times,
and in divers manners, God spake to the fathers by the
prophets, till at length the Lord Jesus himself was manifest
in flesh, and came and tabernacled amongst us.

This first promise must certainly be but dark to our first
parents, in comparison of that great light which we enjoy:
and yet, dark as it was, we may assure ourselves they built
upon it their hopes of everlasting salvation, and by that
faith were saved.

How they came to stand in need of this promise, and what

is the extent and meaning of it, I intend, God willing, to make the subject matter of your present meditation.

The fall of man is written in too legible characters not to be understood: Those that deny it, by their denying, prove it. The very heathens confessed and bewailed it; they could see the streams of corruption running through the whole race of mankind, but could not trace them to the fountain-head. Before God gave a revelation of his Son, man was a riddle to himself. And Moses unfolds more, in this one chapter (out of which the text is taken) than all mankind could have been capable of finding out of themselves, though they had studied all eternity.

In the preceding chapter he had given us a full account how God spake the world into being; and especially how he formed man of the dust of the earth, and breathed into him the breath of life, so that he became a living soul. A council of the Trinity was called concerning the formation of this lovely creature. The result of that council was, 'Let us make man in our image, after our likeness. So God created man in his own image, in the image of God created he him'. Moses remarkably repeats these words, that we might take particular notice of our divine Original. Never was so much expressed in so few words: none but a man inspired could have done so. But it is remarkable, that though Moses mentions our being made in the image of God, yet he mentions it but twice, and that in a transient manner; as though he would have said, that 'man was made in honour, God made him upright, "in the image of God, male and female, created he them". But man so soon fell, and became like the beasts that perish, nay, like the devil himself, that it is scarce worth mentioning.'

How soon man fell after he was created, is not told us;

and therefore, to fix any time, is to be wise above what is written, And, I think, they who suppose that man fell the same day in which he was made, have no sufficient ground for their opinion. The many things which are crowded together in the former chapter, such as the formation of Adam's wife, his giving names to the beasts, and his being put into the garden which God had planted, I think require a longer space of time than a day to be transacted in. However, all agree in this, 'man stood not long'. How long, or how short a while, I will not take upon me to determine. It more concerns us to inquire how he came to fall from his steadfastness and what was the rise and progress of the temptation which prevailed over him. The account given us in this chapter concerning it, is very full; and it may do us much service, under God, to make some remarks upon it.

'Now the serpent (says the sacred historian) was more subtil than any beast of the field which the Lord God had made; and he said unto the woman, Yea, hath God said, Ye shall not eat of every tree of the garden?'

Though this was a real serpent, yet he that spake was no other than the devil; from hence, perhaps, called the old serpent, because he took possession of the serpent when he came to beguile our first parents. The devil envied the happiness of man, who was made, as some think, to supply the place of the fallen angels. God made man upright, and with full power to stand if he would. He was just, therefore, in suffering him to be tempted. If he fell, he had no one to blame except himself. But how must Satan effect his fall? He cannot do it by his power, he attempts it therefore by policy: he takes possession of a serpent, which was more subtil than all the beasts of the field which the Lord God

[141]

had made; so that men, who are full of subtilty, but have no piety, are only machines for the devil to work upon just as he pleases.

'And he said unto the woman.' Here is an instance of his subtilty. He says unto the woman, the weaker vessel, and when she was alone from her husband, and therefore was more liable to be overcome; 'Yea, hath God said, Ye shall not eat of every tree in the garden?' These words are certainly spoken in answer to something which the devil either saw or heard. In all probability, the woman was now near the tree of knowledge of good and evil; (for we shall find her, by and by, plucking an apple from it), perhaps she might be looking at it, and wondering what there was in that tree more than the others, that she and her husband should be forbidden to taste of it. Satan seeing this, and coveting to draw her into a parley with him, (for if the devil can persuade us not to resist, but to commune with him, he hath gained a great point), he says, 'Yea, hath God said, ye shall not eat of every tree of the garden?' The first thing he does is to persuade her, if possible, to entertain hard thoughts of God : this is his general way of dealing with God's children : 'Yea, hath God said, ye shall not eat of every tree of the garden? What! hath God planted a garden, and placed you in the midst of it, only to tease and perplex you? hath he planted a garden, and yet forbad you making use of any of the fruits of it at all?' It was impossible for him to ask a more ensnaring question in order to gain his end; for Eve was here seemingly obliged to answer, and vindicate God's goodness. And therefore :

Verses 2, 3. The woman said unto the serpent, 'We may eat of the fruit of the trees of the garden : but of the fruit of the tree which is in the midst of the garden, God hath said, Ye shall not eat of it, neither shall ye touch it, lest ye die'.

The former part of the answer was good, 'We may eat of the fruit of the trees of the garden; God has not forbad us eating of every tree of the garden. No; we may eat of the fruit of the trees in the garden, (and, it should seem, even of the tree of life, which was as a sacrament to man in a state of innocence;) there is only one tree in the midst of the garden, of which God hath said, ye shall not eat of it, neither shall ye touch it, lest ye die'. Here she begins to warp, and sin begins to conceive in her heart. Already she has contracted some of the serpent's poison, by talking with him, which she ought not to have done at all. For she might easily suppose, that it could be no good being that could put such a question unto her, and insinuate such dishonourable thoughts of God. She should therefore have fled from him, and not stood to have parleyed with him at all. Immediately the ill effects of it appear, she begins to soften the divine threatening. God had said, 'The day thou eatest thereof, *thou shalt surely die*'; or, 'dying thou shalt die'. But Eve says, 'Ye shall not eat of it, neither shall ye touch it, *lest ye die*'. We may be assured we are fallen into, and begin to fall by temptation, when we begin to think God will not be as good as his word, in respect to the execution of his threatenings denounced against sin. Satan knew this, and therefore artfully said unto woman, (verse 4.) in an insinuating manner, 'Ye shall not surely die. Surely, God will not be so cruel as to damn you only for eating an apple; it cannot be'. Alas! how many does Satan lead captive at his will, by flattering them, that they shall not surely die; that hell-torments will not be eternal; that God is all mercy; that he therefore will not punish a few years' sin with an eternity

[143]

of misery? But Eve found God as good as his word; and so will all they who go on in sin, under a false hope that they shall not surely die.

We may also understand the words spoken positively, and this is agreeable to what follows; 'You shall not surely die; it is all a delusion, a mere bugbear, to keep you in a servile subjection'.

For (verse 5.) 'God doth know, that in the day ye eat thereof, then shall your eyes be opened, and ye shall be as gods, knowing good and evil.'

What child of God can expect to escape slander, when God himself was thus slandered even in paradise? Surely the understanding of Eve must have been, in some measure, blinded, or she would not have suffered the tempter to speak such perverse things. In what odious colours is God here represented! 'God doth know, that in the day ye eat thereof, ye shall be as gods', (equal with God). So that the grand temptation was, that they should be hereafter under no control, equal, if not superior, to God that made them, knowing good and evil. Eve could not tell what Satan meant by this; but, to be sure, she understood it of some great privilege which they were to enjoy. And thus Satan now points out a way which seems right to sinners, but does not tell them the end of that way is death.

To give strength and force to this temptation, in all probability, Satan, or the serpent, at this time plucked an apple from the tree, and ate it before Eve; by which Eve might be induced to think, that the sagacity and power of speech, which the serpent had above the other beasts, must be owing, in a great measure, to his eating that fruit; and therefore, if he received so much improvement, she might also expect a like benefit from it. All this, I think, is clear;

for otherwise, I do not see with what propriety it could be said, 'When the woman saw that it was good for food'. How could she know it was good for food, unless she had seen the serpent feed upon it.

Satan now begins to get ground apace. Lust had conceived in Eve's heart; shortly it will bring forth sin. Sin being conceived, brings forth death. Verse 6. 'And when the woman saw that the tree was good for food, and that it was pleasant to the eyes, and a tree to be desired to make one wise, she took of the fruit thereof, and did eat, and gave also unto her husband, and he did eat.'

Our senses are the landing ports of our spiritual enemies. How needful is that resolution of holy Job, 'I have made a covenant with mine eyes!' When Eve began to gaze on the forbidden fruit with her eyes, she soon began to long after it with her heart. When she saw that it was good for food, and pleasant to the eyes, (here was the lust of the flesh, and lust of the eye), but, above all, a tree to be desired to make one wise, wiser than God would have her be, nay, as wise as God himself; she took of the fruit thereof, and gave also unto her husband with her, and he did eat. As soon as ever she sinned herself, she turned tempter to her husband. It is dreadful when those who should be help-meets for each other in the great work of their salvation, are only promoters of each other's damnation: if we do evil, we shall entice others to do evil also. There is a close connection between doing and teaching. How needful then is it for us all to take heed that we do not sin any way ourselves, lest we should become factors for the devil, and ensnare, perhaps, our nearest and dearest relatives? 'She gave also unto her husband with her, and he did eat.'

Alas! what a complication of crimes was there in this one

single act of sin! Here is an utter disbelief of God's threatening; the utmost ingratitude to their Maker, who had so lately planted this garden, and placed them in it, with such a glorious and comprehensive charter; and the utmost neglect of their posterity, who they knew were to stand or fall with them. Here was the utmost pride of heart: they wanted to be equal with God. Here is the utmost contempt put upon his threatening and his law: the devil is credited and obeyed before him, and all this only to satisfy their sensual appetite. Never was a crime of such a complicated nature committed by any here below: nothing but the devil's apostacy and rebellion could equal it.

And what are the consequences of their disobedience? Are their eyes opened? Yes, their eyes are opened; but, alas! it is only to see their own nakedness. For we are told (verse 7.) 'That the eyes of them both were opened, and they knew that they were naked.' Naked of God, naked of every thing that was holy and good, and destitute of the divine image, which they before enjoyed. They might rightly now be termed *Ichabod*; for the glory of the Lord had departed from them. O how low did these sons of the morning then fall! out of God, into themselves; from being partakers of the divine nature, into the nature of the devil and the beast. Well, therefore, might they know that they were naked, not only in body, but in soul.

And how do they behave, now they are naked? Do they flee to God for pardon? Do they seek to God for a robe to cover their nakedness? No, they were now dead to God, and became earthly, sensual, devilish: therefore, instead of applying for God's mercy, 'they sewed or platted fig-leaves together, and made themselves aprons', or things to gird about them. This is a lively representation of all natural men: we see that we are naked; we, in some measure, confess it; but instead of looking up to God for succour, we patch up a righteousness of our own, (as our first parents platted fig-leaves together) hoping to cover our nakedness by that. But our righteousness will not stand the severity of God's judgment; it will do us no more service than the fig-leaves did Adam and Eve, that is, none at all.

For (verse 8) 'They heard the voice of the Lord God walking in the trees of the garden in the cool of the day; and Adam and his wife (notwithstanding their fig-leaves) hid themselves from the presence of the Lord God among the trees of the garden.'

They heard the voice of the Lord God, or the Word of the Lord God, even the Lord Jesus Christ, who is 'the Word that was with God, and the Word that was God'. They heard him walking in the trees of the garden in the cool of the day. A season, perhaps, when Adam and Eve used to go, in an especial manner, and offer up an evening-sacrifice of praise and thanksgiving. The cool of the day! Perhaps the sin was committed early in the morning, or at noon; but God would not come upon them immediately, he stayed till the cool of the day. And if we would effectually reprove others, we should not do it when they are warmed with passion, but wait till the cool of the day.

But what an alteration is here! Instead of rejoicing at the voice of their beloved, instead of meeting him with open arms and enlarged hearts, as before, they now hide themselves in the trees of the garden. Alas! what a foolish attempt was this? Surely they must be naked, otherwise how could they think of hiding themselves from God? Whither could they flee from his presence? But, by their fall, they had contracted an enmity against God: they now hated,

[147]

and were afraid to converse with, God their Maker. And is not this our case by nature? Assuredly it is. We labour to cover our nakedness with the fig-leaves of our own righteousness: we hide ourselves from God as long as we can, and will not come, and never should come, did not the Father prevent, draw, and sweetly constrain us by his grace, as he here prevented Adam.

Verse 9. 'And the Lord God called unto Adam, and said unto him, Adam, where art thou?'

'The Lord God called unto Adam,' (for otherwise Adam would never have called unto the Lord God,) and said, 'Adam, where art thou? How is it that thou comest not to pay thy devotions as usual?' Christians, remember the Lord keeps an account when you fail coming to worship. Whenever therefore you are tempted to withhold your attendance, let each of you fancy you hear the Lord God calling unto you, and saying, 'O man, O woman, where art thou?' It may be understood in another and better sense; 'Adam, where art thou?' What a condition is thy poor soul in? This is the first thing the Lord asks and convinces a sinner of, when he prevents and calls him effectually by his grace; he also calls him by name, for unless God speaks to us in particular, and we know where we are, how poor, how miserable, how blind, how naked, we shall never value the redemption wrought out for us by the death and obedience of the dear Lord Jesus. 'Adam, where art thou?'

Verse 10. 'And he said, I heard thy voice in the garden, and I was afraid.' See what cowards sin makes us. If we knew no sin, we should know no fear. 'Because I was naked, and I hid myself.'

Verse 11. 'And he said, who told thee that thou wast naked? Hast thou eaten of the tree, whereof I (thy Maker and

Lawgiver) commanded thee that thou shouldest not eat?'

God knew very well that Adam was naked, and that he had eaten of the forbidden fruit. But God would know it from Adam's own mouth. Thus God knows all our necessities before we ask, but yet insists upon our asking for his grace, and confessing our sins. For, by such acts, we acknowledge our dependence upon God, take shame to ourselves, and thereby give glory to his great name.

Verse 12. 'And the man said, The woman which thou gavest to be with me, she gave me of the tree, and I did eat.'

Never was nature more lively delineated. See what pride Adam contracted by the fall! How unwilling he is to lay the blame upon, or take shame to, himself. This answer is full of insolence towards God, enmity against his wife, and disingenuity in respect to himself. For herein he tacitly reflects upon God. 'The woman that *thou* gavest to be with me.' As much as to say, If *thou* hadst not given me *that woman*, I had not eaten the forbidden fruit. Thus, when men sin, they lay the fault upon their passions. Their language is, 'The appetites that thou gavest us, they deceived us; and therefore we sinned against thee'. But as God, notwithstanding, punished Adam for hearkening to the voice of his wife, so he will punish those who hearken to the dictates of their corrupt inclinations: for God compels no man to sin. Adam might have withstood the solicitations of his wife, if he would. And so, if we look up to God, we should find grace to help in the time of need. The devil and our own hearts tempt, but they cannot force us to consent, without the concurrence of our own will. So that our damnation is of ourselves, as it will evidently appear at the great day, notwithstanding all men's present impudent replies against God. As Adam speaks insolently in respect to God, so he speaks with enmity against his wife; the woman, or this woman, she gave me. He lays all the fault upon her, and speaks of her with much contempt. He does not say, my wife, my dear wife; but *this woman*. Sin disunites the most united hearts: it is the bane of holy fellowship. Those who have been companions in sin here, if they die without repentance, will both hate and condemn one another hereafter. All damned souls are accusers of their brethren. Thus it is, in some degree, on this side the grave. 'The woman whom thou gavest to be with me, she gave me of the tree, and I did eat.' What a disingenuous speech was here! He makes use of no less than fifteen words to excuse himself, and but one or two (in the original) to confess his fault, if it may be called a confession at all. 'The woman whom thou gavest to be with me, she gave me of the tree'; here are fifteen words; 'and I did eat'. With what reluctance do these last words come out! How soon are they uttered! 'And I did eat.' But thus it is with an unhumbled, unregenerate heart: it will be laying the fault upon the dearest friend in the world, nay, upon God himself, rather than take shame to itself. This pride we are all subject to by the fall; and till our hearts are broken, and made contrite by the Spirit of our Lord Jesus Christ, we shall be always charging God foolishly. 'Against thee, and thee only, have I sinned, that thou mightest be justified in thy saying, and clear when thou art judged', is the language of none but those, who, like David, are willing to confess their faults, and are truly sorry for their sins. This was not the case with Adam; his heart was not broken; and therefore he lays the fault of his disobedience upon his wife and God, and not upon himself; 'The woman whom thou gavest to be with me, she gave me of the tree, and I did eat'.

Verse 13. 'And the Lord God said unto the woman, What is this that thou hast done?' What a wonderful concern does God express in this expostulation! 'What a deluge of misery hast thou brought upon thyself, thy husband, and thy posterity? What is this that thou hast done? Disobeyed thy God, obeyed the devil, and ruined thy husband, for whom I made thee to be an help-meet! What is this that thou hast done?' God would here awaken her to a sense of her crime and danger, and therefore, as it were, thunders in her ears; for the law must be preached to self-righteous sinners. We must take care of healing before we see sinners wounded, lest we should say, Peace, peace, where there is no peace. Secure sinners must hear the thunderings of mount Sinai, before we bring them to mount Zion. They who never preach up the law, it is to be feared, are unskilful in delivering the glad tidings of the gospel. Every minister should be a *Boanerges*, a son of thunder, as well as a *Barnabas*, a son of consolation. There was an earthquake and a whirlwind, before the small still voice came to Elijah: we must first shew people they are condemned, and then shew them how they must be saved. But how and when to preach the law, and when to apply the promises of the gospel, wisdom is profitable to direct. 'And the Lord God said unto the woman, What is this that thou hast done?'

'And the woman said, The serpent beguiled me, and I did eat.' She does not make use of so many words to excuse herself, as her husband; but her heart is as unhumbled as his. What is this, says God, that thou hast done? God here charges her with doing it. She dares not deny the fact, or say, I have not done it; but she takes all the blame off herself, and lays it upon the serpent; 'The serpent beguiled me, and I did eat.' She does not say, 'Lord, I was to blame for talking with the serpent; Lord, I did wrong in not hastening to my husband when he put the first question to me; Lord, I plead guilty, I only am to blame, O let not my poor husband suffer for my wickedness!' This would have been the language of her heart, had she now been a true penitent. But both were now alike proud; therefore neither will lay the blame upon themselves: 'The serpent beguiled me, and I did eat — The woman which thou gavest to be with me, she gave me of the tree, and I did eat.'

I have been the more particular in remarking this part of their behaviour because it tends so much to the magnifying of free-grace, and plainly shews us that salvation cometh only from the Lord. Let us take a short view of the miserable circumstances our first parents were now in: They were legally and spiritually dead, children of wrath, and heirs of hell. They had eaten the fruit, of which God had commanded them that they should not eat; and when arraigned before God, notwithstanding their crime was so complicated, they could not be brought to confess it. What reason can be given why sentence of death should not be pronounced against the prisoners at the bar? All must own they are worthy to die. Nay, how can God, consistently with his justice, possibly forgive them? He had threatened, that the day wherein they ate of the forbidden fruit, they should 'surely die'; and, if he did not execute this threatening, the devil might then slander the Almighty indeed. And yet mercy cries, Spare these sinners, spare the work of thine own hands. Behold, then, wisdom contrives a scheme how God may be just, and yet be merciful; be faithful to his threatening, punish the offence, and at the same time spare the offender. An amazing scene of divine love here opens to our view, which had been from all eternity hid in the heart of

God! Notwithstanding Adam and Eve were thus un-humbled, and did not so much as put up one single petition for pardon, God immediately passes sentence upon the serpent, and reveals to them a Saviour.

Verse 14. 'And the Lord God said unto the serpent, Because thou hast done this, thou art cursed above all cattle, and above every beast of the field; upon thy belly shalt thou go, and dust shalt thou eat all the days of thy life;' that is, he should be in subjection, and his power should always be limited and restrained. 'His enemies shall lick the very dust,' says the Psalmist.

Verse 15. 'And I will put enmity between thee and the woman, and between thy seed and her seed: it shall bruise thy head, and thou shalt bruise his heel.'

Before I proceed to the explanation of this verse, I cannot but take notice of one great mistake which the author of the *Whole Duty of Man* is guilty of, in making this verse contain a covenant between God and Adam, as though God now personally treated with Adam, as before the fall. For talking of the second covenant in his preface, concerning caring for the soul, says he, 'This second covenant was made with Adam, and us in him, presently after the fall, and is briefly contained in these words, Gen 3.15, where God declares, "The seed of the woman shall break the serpent's head"; and this was made up, as the first was, of some mercies to be afforded by God, and some duties to be performed by us'. This is exceedingly false divinity; for these words are not spoken to Adam; they are directed only to the serpent. Adam and Eve stood by as criminals, and God could not treat with them, because they had broken his covenant. And it is so far from being a covenant wherein 'some mercies are to be afforded by God, and some duties to be performed by

[153]

us', that here is not a word looking that way; it is only a declaration of a free gift of salvation through Jesus Christ our Lord. God the Father and God the Son had entered into a covenant concerning the salvation of the elect from all eternity, wherein God the Father promised, that, if the Son would offer his soul a sacrifice for sin, he should see his seed. Now this is an open revelation of this secret covenant, and therefore God speaks in the most positive terms, 'It shall bruise thy head, and thou shalt bruise his heel'. The first Adam, God had treated with before; he proved false: God therefore, to secure the second covenant from being broken, puts it into the hands of the second Adam, the Lord from heaven. Adam, after the fall, stood no longer as our representative; he and Eve were only private persons, as we are, and were only to lay hold on the declaration of mercy contained in this promise, by faith, (as they really did), and by that they were saved. I do not say but we are to believe and obey, if we are everlastingly saved. Faith and obedience are conditions, if we only mean that they in order go before our salvation; but I deny that these are proposed by God to Adam, or that God treats with him in this promise, as he did before the fall under the covenant of works. For how could that be, when Adam and Eve were now prisoners at the bar, without strength to perform any conditions at all? The truth is this: God, as a reward of Christ's sufferings, promised to give the elect faith and repentance, in order to bring them to eternal life: and both these, and every thing else necessary for their everlasting happiness, are infallibly secured to them in this promise; as Mr Boston, an excellent Scots divine, clearly shews, in a book entitled, 'A view of the covenant of grace'.

This is by no means an unnecessary distinction; it is a

matter of great importance: for want of knowing this, people have been so long misled. They have been taught that they must do so and so, as though they were under a covenant of works, and then for DOING this, they should be saved. Whereas, on the contrary, people should be taught, That the Lord Jesus was the second Adam, with whom the Father entered into covenant for fallen man; that they can now do nothing of or for themselves, and should therefore come to God beseeching him to give them faith, by which they shall be enabled to lay hold on the righteousness of Christ; and that faith they will then shew forth by their works, out of love and gratitude to the ever blessed Jesus, their most glorious redeemer, for what he has done for their souls. This is a consistent scriptural scheme; without holding this, we must run into one of those two bad extremes; I mean, Antinomianism on the one hand, or Arminianism on the other: from both which may the good Lord deliver us!

But to proceed: By the seed of the woman, we are here to understand the Lord Jesus Christ, who, though very God of very God, was, for us men and our salvation, to have a body prepared for him by the Holy Ghost, and to be born of a woman who had never known man, and by his obedience and death make an atonement for man's transgression, and bring in an everlasting righteousness, work in them a new nature, and thereby bruise the serpent's head, that is, destroy his power and dominion over them. By the serpent's seed, we are to understand the devil and all his children, who are permitted by God to tempt and sift *his* children. But, blessed be God, he can reach no further than our heel.

It is not to be doubted but Adam and Eve understood this promise in this sense; for it is plain, in the latter part of the chapter, sacrifices were instituted. From whence should those skins come, but from beasts slain for sacrifice, of which God made them coats? We find Abel, as well as Cain, offering sacrifice in the next chapter: and the apostle tells us he did it by faith, no doubt, in this promise. And Eve, when Cain, was born, said, 'I have gotten a man from the Lord'; or, (as Mr Henry observes it may be rendered), 'I have gotten a man – the Lord – the promised Messiah'. Some further suppose, that Eve was the first believer; and therefore they translate it thus, 'The seed of *this* (not *the*) woman': which magnifies the grace of God so much the more, that she, who was first in the transgression, should be the first partaker of redemption. Adam believed also, and was saved: for unto Adam and his wife did the Lord God make coats of skins, and clothed them: which was a remarkable type of their being clothed with the righteousness of our Lord Jesus Christ.

This promise was literally fulfilled in the person of our Lord Jesus Christ. Satan bruised his heel, when he tempted him for forty days together in the wilderness: he bruised his heel, when he raised up strong persecution against him during the time of his public ministry; he in an especial manner bruised his heel, when our Lord complained, that his soul was exceedingly sorrowful, even unto death, and he sweat great drops of blood falling upon the ground, in the garden: he bruised his heel, when he put it into the heart of Judas to betray him: and he bruised him yet most of all, when his emissaries nailed him to an accursed tree, and our Lord cried out, 'My God, my God, why hast thou forsaken me?' Yet in all this, the blessed Jesus, the seed of the woman, bruised Satan's accursed head: for, in that he was tempted, he was able to succour those that are tempted.

By his stripes we are healed. The chastisement of our peace was upon him. By dying, he destroyed him that had the power of death, that is, the devil. He thereby spoiled principalities and powers, and made a shew of them openly, triumphing over them upon the cross.

This promise has been fulfilled in the elect of God, considered collectively, as well before, as since the coming of our Lord in the flesh: for they may be called the seed of the woman. Marvel not, that all who live godly in Christ Jesus, must suffer persecution. In this promise, there is an eternal enmity put between the seed of the woman, and the seed of the serpent; so that those that are born after the flesh, cannot but persecute those that are born after the spirit. This enmity shewed itself, soon after this promise was revealed, in Cain's bruising the heel of Abel: it continued in the church through all ages before Christ came in the flesh, as the history of the Bible, and the 11th chapter of the Hebrews, plainly shew. It raged exceedingly after our Lord's ascension; witness the Acts of the Apostles, and the history of the primitive Christians. It now rages, and will continue to rage and shew itself, in a greater or less degree, to the end of time. But let not this dismay us, for in all this, the seed of the woman is more than conqueror, and bruises the serpent's head. Thus the Israelites, the more they were oppressed, the more they increased. Thus it was with the apostles; thus it was with their immediate followers. So that Tertullian compares the church in his time to a mowed field; the more frequently it is cut, the more it grows. The blood of the martyrs was always the seed of the church. And I have often sat down with wonder and delight, and admired how God has made the very schemes which his enemies contrived, in order to hinder, become the most effectual means to propagate his gospel. The devil has had so little success in persecution, that if I did not know that he and his children, according to this verse, could not but persecute, I should think he would count it his strength to sit still. What did he get by persecuting the martyrs in queen Mary's time? Was not the grace of God exceedingly glorified in their support? What did he get by persecuting the good old Puritans? Did it not prove the peopling of New England? Or, to come near our own times, what has he got by putting *us* out of the synagogues? Hath not the Word of God, since that, mightily prevailed? My dear hearers, you must excuse me for enlarging on this head; God fills my soul generally, when I come to this topic. I can say with Luther, 'If it were not for persecution, I should not understand the scripture'. If Satan should be suffered to bruise my heel further, and his servants should thrust me into prison, I doubt not but even that would tend only to the more effectual bruising of his head. I remember a saying of the Lord Chancellor to the pious Bradford: 'Thou hast done more hurt', said he, 'by thy exhortations in private in prison, than thou didst in preaching before thou wast put in', or words to this effect. The promise of the text is my daily support; 'I will put enmity between thy seed and her seed; it shall bruise thy head, and thou shalt bruise his heel'.

Further: this promise is also fulfilled, not only in the church in general, but in every individual believer in particular. In every believer there are two seeds, the seed of the woman, and the seed of the serpent; the flesh lusting against the spirit, and the spirit against the flesh. It is with the believer, when quickened with grace in his heart, as it was with Rebekah, when she had conceived Esau and Jacob in her womb; she felt a struggling, and began to be uneasy;

'If it be so', says she, 'why am I thus?' Thus grace and nature struggle (if I may so speak) in the womb of a believer's heart: but, as it was there said, 'The elder shall serve the younger'; so it is here, — grace in the end shall get the better of nature; the seed of the woman shall bruise the serpent's head. Many of you that have believed in Christ, perhaps may find some particular corruption yet strong, so strong, that you are sometimes ready to cry out with David, 'I shall fall one day by the hand of Saul'. But, fear not, the promise in the text ensures the perseverance and victory of believers over sin, Satan, death, and hell. What if indwelling corruption does yet remain, and the seed of the serpent bruise your heel, in vexing and disturbing your righteous souls? Fear not, though faint, yet pursue: you shall yet bruise the serpent's head. Christ hath died for you; and yet a little while, and he will send death to destroy the very being of sin in you. Which brings me — To shew the most extensive manner in which the promise of the text shall be fulfilled, viz. at the final judgment, when the Lord Jesus shall present the elect to his Father, without spot or wrinkle, or any such thing, glorified both in body and soul.

Then shall the seed of the woman give the last and fatal blow, in bruising the serpent's head. Satan, the accuser of the brethren, and all his accursed seed, shall then be cast out, and never suffered to disturb the seed of the woman any more. Then shall the righteous shine as the sun in the kingdom of their Father, and sit with Christ on thrones in majesty on high.

Let us, therefore, not be weary of well-doing; for we shall reap an eternal harvest of comfort, if we faint not. Dare, dare, my dear brethren in Christ, to follow the Captain of your salvation, who was made perfect through sufferings.

The seed of the woman shall bruise the serpent's head. Fear not men. Be not too much cast down at the deceitfulness of your hearts. Fear not devils; you shall get the victory even over them. The Lord Jesus has engaged to make you more than conquerors over all. Plead with your Saviour, plead: plead the promise in the text. Wrestle, wrestle with God in prayer. If it has been given you to believe, fear not if it should also be given you to suffer. Be not anywise terrified by your adversaries; the King of the church has them all in a chain: be kind to them; pray for them; but fear them not. The Lord will yet bring back his ark, though at present driven into the wilderness; and Satan like lightning shall fall from heaven.

Are there any enemies of God here? The promise of the text encourages me to bid you defiance: the seed of the woman, the ever blessed Jesus, shall bruise the serpent's head. What signifies all your malice? You are only raging waves of the sea, foaming out your own shame. For you, without repentance, is reserved the blackness of darkness for ever. The Lord Jesus sits in heaven, ruling over all, and causing all things to work for his children's good; he laughs you to scorn: he hath you in the utmost derision, and therefore so will I. Who are you that persecute the children of the ever-blessed God? Though a poor stripling, the Lord Jesus, the seed of the woman, will enable me to bruise your heads.

My brethren in Christ, I think I do not speak thus in my own strength, but in the strength of my Redeemer. I know in whom I have believed: I am persuaded he will keep that safe, which I have committed unto him. He is faithful, who hath promised that the seed of the woman shall bruise the serpent's head. May we all experience a daily completion of this promise, both in the church and in our hearts, till we come to the church of the first-born, the spirits of just men made perfect, in the presence and actual fruition of the great God our heavenly Father.

To whom, with the Son, and the Holy Ghost, be ascribed all honour, power, might, majesty, and dominion, now and for evermore. *Amen.*

WALKING WITH GOD

And Enoch walked with God: and he was not; for God
took him. *Gen* 5.24

Various are the pleas and arguments which men of corrupt
minds frequently urge against yielding obedience to the just
and holy commands of God. But, perhaps, one of the most
common objections that they make is this, that our Lord's
commands are not practicable, because contrary to flesh and
blood; and consequently, that he is 'an hard master, reaping
where he has not sown, and gathering where he has not
strewed'. These we find were the sentiments entertained by
that wicked and slothful servant mentioned in the 25th of
St Matthew; and are undoubtedly the same with many
which are maintained in the present wicked and adulterous
generation. The Holy Ghost foreseeing this, hath taken care
to inspire holy men of old, to record the examples of many
holy men and women; who, even under the Old Testament
dispensation, were enabled cheerfully to take Christ's yoke
upon them, and counted his service perfect freedom. The
large catalogue of saints, confessors, and martyrs, drawn up
in the 11th chapter to the Hebrews, abundantly evidences
the truth of this observation. What a great cloud of witnesses have we there presented to our view? All eminent
for their faith, but some shining with a greater degree of
lustre than do others. The proto-martyr Abel leads the van.

And next to him we find Enoch mentioned, not only because he was next in order of time, but also on account of his exalted piety; he is spoken of in the words of the text in a very extraordinary manner. We have here a short but very full and glorious account, both of his behaviour in this world, and the triumphant manner of his entry into the next. The former is contained in these words, 'And Enoch walked with God'. The latter in these, 'and he was not: for God took him'. He was not; that is, he was not found, he was not taken away in the common manner, he did not see death; for God had translated him. (Heb 11.5. Who this Enoch was, does not appear so plainly. To me, he seems to have been a person of public character; I suppose, like Noah, a preacher of righteousness. And, if we may credit the apostle Jude, he was a flaming preacher. For he quotes one of his prophecies, wherein he saith, 'Behold, the Lord cometh with ten thousands of his saints, to execute judgment upon all, and to convince all that are ungodly among them, of all their ungodly deeds which they have ungodly committed, and of all their hard speeches, which ungodly sinners have spoken against him'. But whether a public or private person, he has a noble testimony given him in the lively oracles. The author of the epistle to the Hebrews saith, that before his translation he had this testimony, 'that he pleased God'; and his being translated, was a proof of it beyond all doubt. And I would observe, that it was wonderful wisdom in God to translate Enoch and Elijah under the Old Testament dispensation, that hereafter, when it should be asserted that the Lord Jesus was carried into heaven, it might not seem a thing altogether incredible to the Jews; since they themselves confessed that two of their own prophets had been translated several hundred years before. But it is not my design to detain you any longer, by enlarging, or making observations, on Enoch's short but comprehensive character: the thing I have in view being to give a discourse, as the Lord shall enable, upon a weighty and a very important subject; I mean, *walking with God.* 'And Enoch walked with God.' If so much as this can be truly said of you and me after our decease, we shall not have any reason to complain that we have lived in vain.

In handling my intended subject, I shall,

First, Endeavour to shew what is implied in these words, *walked with God.*

Secondly, I shall prescribe some means, upon the due observance of which, believers may keep up and maintain their *walk with God.* And,

Thirdly, Offer some motives to stir us up, if we never walked with God before, to come and walk with God now. The whole shall be closed with a word or two of application.

First, I am to shew what is implied in these words, 'walked with God'; or, in other words, what we are to understand by *walking with God.*

And *First, Walking with God* implies, that the prevailing power of the enmity of a person's heart be taken away by the blessed Spirit of God. Perhaps it may seem a hard saying to some, but our own experience daily proves what the scriptures in many places assert, that the carnal mind, the mind of the unconverted natural man, nay, the mind of the regenerate, so far as any part of him remains unrenewed, is enmity, not only an enemy, but enmity itself, against God; so that it is not subject to the law of God, neither indeed can it be. Indeed, one may well wonder that any creature, especially that lovely creature man, made after his Maker's

own image, should ever have any enmity, much less a prevailing enmity, against that very God in whom he lives, and
moves, and hath his being. But alas! so it is. Our first
parents contracted it when they fell from God by eating the
forbidden fruit, and the bitter and malignant contagion of
it hath descended to, and quite overspread, their whole posterity. This enmity discovered itself in Adam's endeavouring
to hide himself in the trees of the garden. When he heard
the voice of the Lord God, instead of running with an open
heart, saying Here I am; alas! he now wanted no communion with God; and still more discovered his lately contracted enmity, by the excuse he made to the Most High:
'The woman (or, this woman) thou gavest to be with me, she
gave me of the tree, and I did eat'. By saying thus, he in
effect lays all the fault upon God; as though he had said,
If thou hadst not given me this woman, I had not sinned
against thee, so thou mayest thank thyself for my transgression. In the same manner this enmity works in the
hearts of Adam's children. They now and again find something rising against God, and saying even unto God, What
doest thou? 'It scorns any meaner competitor (says the
learned Dr Owen, in his excellent treatise on indwelling sin)
than God himself.' Its command is like that of the Assyrians
in respect to Ahab – shoot only at the king. And it strikes
against every thing that has the appearance of real piety, as
the Assyrians shot at Jehoshaphat in his royal clothes. But
the opposition ceases when it finds that it is only an appearance, as the Assyrians left off shooting at Jehoshaphat, when
they perceived it was not Ahab they were shooting at. This
enmity discovered itself in accursed Cain; he hated and
slew his brother Abel, because Abel loved, and was pecu-
liarly favoured by, his God. And this same enmity rules and

prevails in every man that is naturally engendered of the offspring of Adam. Hence that averseness to prayer and holy duties which we find in children, and very often in grown persons, who have notwithstanding been blessed with a religious education. And all that open sin and wickedness, which like a deluge has overflowed the world, are only so many streams running from this dreadful contagious fountain; I mean the enmity of man's desperately wicked and deceitful heart. He that cannot set his seal to this, knows nothing yet, in a saving manner, of the Holy Scriptures, or of the power of God. And all that do know this, will readily acknowledge, that before a person can be said to walk with God, the prevailing power of this heart-enmity must be destroyed: for persons do not use to walk and keep company together, who entertain an irreconcilable enmity and hatred against one another. Observe me, I say, the prevailing power of this enmity must be taken away; for the in-being of it will never be totally removed, till we bow down our heads, and give up the ghost. The apostle Paul, no doubt, speaks of himself, and that, too, not when he was a Pharisee, but a real Christian; when he complains, 'that when he would do good, evil was present with him'; not having dominion over him, but opposing and resisting his good intentions and actions, so that he could not do the things which he would, in that perfection which the new man desired. This is what he calls sin dwelling in him. 'And this is that Φρόνημα σαρκος, which (to use the words of the ninth article of our church,) some do expound the wisdom, some sensuality, some the affectation, some the desire, of the flesh, which doth remain, yea, in them that are regenerated.' But as for its prevailing power, it is destroyed in every soul that is truly born of God, and gradually more and more weakened as the believer grows in grace, and the Spirit of God gains a greater and greater ascendancy in the heart.

But *Secondly*, Walking with God not only implies, that the prevailing power of the enmity of a man's heart be taken away, but also that a person is actually reconciled to God the Father, in and through the all-sufficient righteousness and atonement of his dear Son. 'Can two walk together, (says Solomon,[1]) unless they are agreed?' Jesus is our peace as well as our peace-maker. When we are justified by faith in Christ, then, but not till then, we have peace with God; and consequently cannot be said till then to walk with him, walking with a person being a sign and token that we are friends to that person, or at least, though we have been at variance, yet that now we are reconciled and become friends again. This is the great errand that gospel ministers are sent out upon. To us is committed the ministry of reconciliation; as ambassadors for God, we are to beseech sinners, in Christ's stead, to be reconciled unto God, and when they comply with the gracious invitation, and are actually by faith brought into a state of reconciliation with God, then, and not till then, may they be said so much as to begin to walk with God.

Further, *Thirdly*, Walking with God implies a settled abiding communion and fellowship with God, or what in scripture is called, 'The Holy Ghost dwelling in us'. This is what our Lord promised when he told his disciples that 'the Holy Spirit should be in and with them'; not to be like a wayfaring man, to stay only for a night, but to reside and make his abode in their hearts. This, I am apt to believe, is what the apostle John would have us understand, when he talks of a person 'abiding in him, in Christ, and walking as he himself also walked'. And this is what is particularly

[1] The reference is in fact to Amos 3:3.

[167]

meant in the words of our text. 'And Enoch walked with God', that is, he kept up and maintained a holy, settled, habitual, though undoubtedly not altogether uninterrupted communion and fellowship with God, in and through Christ Jesus. So that to sum up what has been said on this part of the first general head, *walking with God* consists especially in the fixed habitual bent of the will for God, in an habitual dependence upon his power and promise, in an habitual voluntary dedication of our all to his glory, in an habitual eyeing of his precept in all we do, and in an habitual complacence in his pleasure in all we suffer.

Fourthly, Walking with God implies our making progress or advances in the divine life. *Walking*, in the very first idea of the word, seems to suppose a progressive motion. A person that walks, though he move slowly, yet he goes forward, and does not continue in one place. And so it is with those that walk with God. They go on, as the Psalmist says, 'from strength to strength'; or, in the language of the apostle Paul, 'they pass from glory to glory, even by the Spirit of the Lord'. Indeed, in one sense, the divine life admits of neither increase nor decrease. When a soul is born of God, to all intents and purposes he is a child of God; and though he should live to the age of Methuselah, yet he would then be only a child of God after all. But in another sense, the divine life admits of decays and additions. Hence it is, that we find the people of God charged with backslidings and losing their first love. And hence it is that we hear of babes, young men, and fathers in Christ. And upon this account it is that the apostle exhorts Timothy, 'to let his progress be made known to all men'. And what is here required of Timothy in particular, by St Peter is enjoined on all Christians in general, 'But grow in grace, (says he), and in the knowledge of our Lord and Saviour Jesus Christ'. For the new creature increases in spiritual stature; and though a person can but be a new creature, yet there are some that are more conformed to the divine image than others, and will after death be admitted to a greater degree of blessedness. For want of observing this distinction, even some gracious souls, that have better hearts than heads, (as well as men of corrupt minds, reprobates concerning the faith) have unawares run into downright Antinomian principles, denying all growth of grace in a believer, or any marks of grace to be laid down in the scriptures of truth. From such principles, and more especially from practices naturally consequent on such principles, may the Lord of all lords deliver us!

From what then has been said, we may now know what is implied in the words, 'walked with God', viz. our having the prevailing enmity of our hearts taken away by the power of the Spirit of God; our being actually reconciled and united to him by faith in Jesus Christ; our having and keeping up a settled communion and fellowship with him; and our making a daily progress in this fellowship, so as to be conformed to the divine image more and more.

How this is done, or, in other words, by what means believers keep up and maintain their walk with God, comes to be considered under our second general head.

And, *First*, Believers keep up and maintain their walk with God by reading of his holy word. 'Search the scriptures', says our blessed Lord, 'for these are they that testify of me'. And the royal Psalmist tells us 'that God's word was a light unto his feet, and a lanthorn unto his paths'; and he makes it one property of a good man, 'that his delight is in the law of the Lord, and that he exercises himself therein day and night'. 'Give thyself to reading', (says Paul to Timothy); 'And this book of the law, (says God to Joshua) shall not go out of thy mouth'. For whatsoever was written aforetime was written for our learning. And the word of God is profitable for reproof, for correction, and for instruction in righteousness, and every way sufficient to make every true child of God thoroughly furnished unto every good work. If we once get above our Bibles, and cease making the written word of God our sole rule both as to faith and practice, we shall soon lie open to all manner of delusion, and be in great danger of making shipwreck of faith and a good conscience. Our blessed Lord, though he had the Spirit of God without measure, yet always was governed by, and fought the devil with, 'It is written'. This the apostle calls the 'sword of the Spirit'. We may say of it, as David said of Goliath's sword, 'None like this'. The scriptures are called the lively oracles of God: not only because they are generally made use of to beget in us a new life, but also to keep up and increase it in the soul. The apostle Peter, in his second epistle, prefers it even to seeing Christ transfigured upon the mount. For after he had said, chap. 1.18. 'This voice which came from heaven we heard, when we were with him in the holy mount'; he adds, 'We have also a more sure word of prophecy; whereunto ye do well that ye take heed, as unto a light shining in a dark place, until the day dawn, and the day-star arise in your hearts': that is, till we shake off these bodies, and see Jesus face to face. Till then we must see and converse with him through the glass of his word. We must make his testimonies our counsellors, and daily, with Mary, sit at Jesus' feet, by faith hearing his word. We shall then by happy experience find, that they are spirit and life, meat indeed and drink indeed, to our souls.

Secondly, Believers keep up and maintain their walk with God by secret prayer. The spirit of grace is always accompanied with the spirit of supplication. It is the very breath of the new creature, the fan of the divine life, whereby the spark of holy fire, kindled in the soul by God, is not only kept in, but raised into a flame. A neglect of secret prayer has been frequently an inlet to many spiritual diseases, and has been attended with fatal consequences. Origen observed, 'That the day he offered incense to an idol, he went out of his closet without making use of secret prayer'. It is one of the most noble parts of the believer's spiritual armour. 'Praying always', says the apostle, 'with all manner of supplication.' 'Watch and pray', says our Lord, 'that ye enter not into temptation.' And he spake a parable, that his disciples should pray, and not faint. Not that our Lord would have us always upon our knees, or in our closets, to the neglect of our other relative duties. But he means, that our souls should be kept in a praying frame, so that we might be able to say, as a good man in Scotland once said to his friends on his death-bed, 'Could these curtains, or could these walls speak, they would tell you what sweet communion I have had with my God here'. O prayer! prayer! It brings and keeps God and man together. It raises man up to God, and brings God down to man. If you would therefore, O believers, keep up your walk with God; pray, pray without ceasing. Be much in secret, set prayer. And when you are about the common business of life, be much in ejaculatory prayer, and send, from time to time, short letters post to heaven upon the wings of faith. They will reach the very heart of God, and return to you again loaded with spiritual blessings.

Thirdly, Holy and frequent meditation is another blessed

means of keeping up a believer's walk with God. 'Prayer, reading, temptation, and meditation', says Luther, 'make a minister.' And they also make and perfect a Christian. Meditation to the soul, is the same as digestion to the body. Holy David found it so, and therefore he was frequently employed in meditation, even in the night season. We read also of Isaac's going out into the fields to meditate in the evening; or, as it is in the margin, to pray. For meditation is a kind of silent prayer, whereby the soul is frequently as it were carried out of itself to God, and in a degree made like unto those blessed spirits, who by a kind of immediate intuition always behold the face of our heavenly Father. None but those happy souls that have been accustomed to this divine employ, can tell what a blessed promoter of the divine life, meditation is. 'Whilst I was musing', says David, 'the fire kindled.' And whilst the believer is musing on the works and word of God, especially that work of works, that wonder of wonders, that mystery of godliness, 'God manifest in the flesh', the Lamb of God slain for the sins of the world, he frequently feels the fire of divine love kindle, so that he is obliged to speak with his tongue, and tell of the loving-kindness of the Lord to his soul. Be frequent therefore in meditation, all ye that desire to keep up and maintain a close and uniform walk with the most high God.

Fourthly, Believers keep up their walk with God, by watching and noting his providential dealings with them. If we believe the scriptures, we must believe what our Lord hath declared therein, 'That the very hairs of his disciples' heads are all numbered; and that a sparrow does not fall to the ground, (either to pick up a grain of corn, or when shot by a fowler), without the knowledge of our heavenly Father'. Every cross has a call in it, and every particular dispensation of divine providence has some particular end to answer in those to whom it is sent. If it be of an afflictive nature, God does thereby say, 'My son, keep thyself from idols': if prosperous, he does, as it were by a small still voice, say, 'My son, give me thy heart'. If believers, therefore, would keep up their walk with God, they must from time to time hear what the Lord has to say concerning them in the voice of his providence. Thus we find that Abraham's servant, when he went to fetch a wife for his master Isaac, eyed and watched the providence of God, and by that means found out the person that was designed for his master's wife. 'For a little hint from providence', says pious Bishop Hall, 'is enough for faith to feed upon.' And as I believe it will be one part of our happiness in heaven, to take a view of, and look back upon, the various links of the golden chain which drew us there; so those that enjoy most of heaven below, I believe, will be the most minute in remarking God's various dealings with them, in respect to his providential dispensations here on earth.

Fifthly, In order to walk closely with God, his children must not only watch the motions of God's providence without them, but the motions also of his blessed Spirit in their hearts. 'As many as are the sons of God, are led by the Spirit of God', and give up themselves to be guided by the Holy Ghost, as a little child gives its hand to be led by a nurse or parent. It is no doubt in this sense that we are to be converted, and become like little children. And though it is the quintessence of enthusiasm, to pretend to be guided by the Spirit without the written word; yet it is every Christian's bounden duty to be guided by the Spirit in conjunction with the written word of God. Watch, therefore, I pray you, O believers, the motions of God's blessed Spirit in your

[173]

souls, and always try the suggestions or impressions that you may at any time feel, by the unerring rule of God's most holy word : and if they are not found to be agreeable to that, reject them as diabolical and delusive. By observing this caution, you will steer a middle course between the two dangerous extremes many of this generation are in danger of running into; I mean, *enthusiasm*, on the one hand, and *deism*, and *downright infidelity*, on the other.

Sixthly, They that would maintain a holy walk with God, must walk with him in ordinances as well as providences, etc. It is therefore recorded of Zachary and Elizabeth, that 'they walked in all God's ordinances, as well as commandments, blameless'. And all rightly informed Christians, will look upon ordinances, not as beggarly elements, but as so many conduit-pipes, whereby the infinitely condescending Jehovah conveys his grace to their souls. They will look upon them as children's bread, and as their highest privileges. Consequently they will be glad when they hear others say, 'Come, let us go up to the house of the Lord'. They will delight to visit the place where God's honour dwelleth, and be very eager to embrace all opportunities to shew forth the Lord Christ's death till he come.

Seventhly and *lastly*, If you would walk with God, you will associate and keep company with those that do walk with him. 'My delight', says holy David, 'is in them that do excel' in virtue. They were, in his sight, the excellent ones of the earth. And the primitive Christians, no doubt, kept up their vigour and first love, by continuing in fellowship one with another. The apostle Paul knew this full well, and therefore exhorts the Christians to see to it, that they did not forsake the assembling of themselves together. For how can one be warm alone? And has not the wisest of men told us, that, 'As iron sharpeneth iron, so doth the countenance of a man his friend?' If we look, therefore, into church history, or make a just observation of our own times, I believe we shall find, that as the power of God prevails, Christian societies, and fellowship meetings prevail proportionably. And as one decays, the other has insensibly decayed and dwindled away at the same time. So necessary is it for those that would walk with God, and keep up the life of religion, to meet together as they have opportunity, in order to provoke one another to love and good works.

Proceed we now to the third general thing proposed: to offer some motives to excite all to come and walk with God.

And, *First*, walking with God is a very honourable thing. This generally is a prevailing motive to persons of all ranks, to stir them up to any important undertaking. O that it may have its due weight and influence with you in respect to the matter now before us! I suppose you would all think it a very high honour to be admitted into an earthly prince's privy council, to be trusted with his secrets, and to have his ear at all times and at all seasons. It seems Haman thought it so, when he boasted, Est 5.11, that besides his being 'advanced above the princes and servants of the king; yea, moreover, Esther the queen did let no man come in with the king unto the banquet that she had prepared, but myself; and to-morrow am I invited unto her also with the king'. And when afterwards a question was put to this same Haman, Chap. 6.6. 'What shall be done unto the man whom the king delighteth to honour?' he answered, verse 8. 'Let the royal apparel be brought which the king used to wear, and the horse that the king rideth upon, and the crown royal which is set upon his head; and let this apparel and horse be delivered to the hand of one of the king's most noble princes, that they may array the man withal whom the king delighteth to honour, and bring him on horseback through the street of the city and proclaim before him, Thus shall it be done to the man whom the king delighteth to honour.' This was all, then, it seems, that an ambitious Haman could ask, and the most valuable thing that he thought Ahasuerus, the greatest monarch upon earth, could give. But, alas, what is this honour in comparison of that which the meanest of those enjoy, that walk with God! Think ye it a small thing, sirs, to have the secret of the Lord of lords with you, and to be called the friends of God? and such honour have all God's saints. The secret of the Lord is with them that fear him: and 'Henceforth (says the blessed Jesus) call I you no longer servants, but friends; for the servant knoweth not the will of his master'. Whatever you may think of it, holy David was so sensible of the honour attending a walk with God, that he declares, 'he had rather be a door-keeper in his house, than to dwell even in the tents of ungodliness'. O that all were like-minded with him!

But, *Secondly*, As it is an honourable, so it is a pleasing thing, to walk with God. The wisest of men has told us, that 'wisdom's ways are ways of pleasantness, and all her paths peace'. And I remember pious Mr Henry, when he was about to expire, said to a friend, 'You have heard many men's dying words, and these are mine: A life spent in communion with God, is the pleasantest life in the world'. I am sure I can set to my seal that this is true. Indeed, I have been listed under Jesus's banner only for a few years; but I have enjoyed more solid pleasure in one moment's communion with my God, than I should or could have enjoyed in the ways of sin, though I had continued to have gone on in them for thousands of years. And may I not appeal to all you that fear and walk with God, for the truth of this? Has not one day in the Lord's courts been better to you than a thousand? In keeping God's commandments, have you not found a present, and very great reward? Has not his word been sweeter to you than the honey or the honeycomb? O what have you felt, when, Jacob-like, you have been wrestling with your God? Has not Jesus often met you when meditating in the fields, and been made known to you over and over again in breaking of bread? Has not the Holy Ghost frequently shed the divine love abroad in your hearts abundantly, and filled you with joy unspeakable, even joy that is full of glory? I know you will answer all these questions in the affirmative, and freely acknowledge the yoke of Christ to be easy, and his burden light; or (to use the words of one of our collects), 'His service is perfect freedom'. And what need we then any further motive to excite us to walk with God?

But methinks I hear some among you say, 'How can these things be? For, if walking with God, as you say, is such an honourable and pleasant thing, whence is it that the name of the people of this way is cast out as evil, and every where spoken against? How comes it to pass that they are frequently afflicted, tempted, destitute, and tormented? Is this the honour, this the pleasure, that you speak of?' I answer, Yes. Stop a while; be not over hasty. Judge not according to appearance, but judge righteous judgment, and all will be well. It is true, we acknowledge the 'people of this way', as you, and Paul before you, when a persecutor, called them, have their names cast out as evil, and are a sect every where spoken against. But by whom? Even by the enemies of the most high God. And do you think it is dis-grace to be spoken evil of by them? Blessed be God, we have not so learned Christ. Our royal Master has pro-nounced those 'blessed, who are persecuted, and have all manner of evil spoken against them falsely'. He has com-manded them 'to rejoice and be exceeding glad', for it is the privilege of their discipleship, and that their reward will be great in heaven. He himself was thus treated. And can there be a greater honour put upon a creature, than to be con-formed to the ever-blessed Son of God? And further, it is equally true that the people of this way are frequently afflicted, tempted, destitute, and tormented. But what of all this? Does this destroy the pleasure of walking with God? No, in no wise; for those that walk with God are enabled, through Christ strengthening them, to joy even in tribula-tion, and to rejoice when they fall into divers temptations. And I believe I may appeal to the experience of all true and close walkers with God, whether or not their suffering times have not frequently been their sweetest times, and that they enjoyed most of God when most cast out and despised by men? This we find was the case of Christ's primitive ser-vants, when threatened by the Jewish sanhedrin, and com-manded to preach no more in the name of Jesus; they rejoiced that they were accounted worthy to suffer shame for the sake of Jesus. Paul and Silas sang praises even in a dungeon; and the face of Stephen, that glorious proto-martyr of the Christian church, shone like the face of an angel. And Jesus is the same now as he was then, and takes care so to sweeten sufferings and afflictions with his love, that his disciples find, by happy experience, that as afflic-tions abound, consolations do much more abound. And therefore these objections, instead of destroying, do only enforce the motives before urged, to excite you to walk with God.

But supposing the objections were just, and walkers with God were as despicable and unhappy as you would represent them to be; yet I have a third motive to offer, which if weighed in the balance of the sanctuary, will over-weigh all objections, viz. That there is a heaven at the end of this walk. For, to use the words of pious bishop Beveridge, 'Though the way be narrow, yet it is not long: and though the gate be strait, yet it opens into everlasting life'. Enoch found it so. He walked with God on earth, and God took him to sit down with him for ever in the kingdom of heaven. Not that we are to expect to be taken away as he was: no, I suppose we shall all die the common death of all men. But after death, the spirits of those who have walked with God shall return to God that gave them; and at the morning of the resurrection, soul and body shall be for ever with the Lord; their bodies shall be fashioned like unto Christ's glorious body, and their souls filled with all the fullness of God. They shall sit on thrones; they shall judge angels. They shall be enabled to sustain an exceeding and eternal weight of glory, even that glory which Jesus Christ enjoyed with the Father before the world began. '*O gloriam quantam et qualem*', said the learned and pious Arndt, just before he bowed down his head, and gave up the ghost. The very thought of it is enough to make us 'wish to leap our seventy years', as good Dr Watts expresses himself, and to make us break out into the earnest language of the royal Psalmist, 'My soul is athirst for God, yea, for the living God. When shall I come to appear in the presence of my God?' I wonder not that a sense of this, when under a more than ordinary irradiation and influx of divine life and love, causes some persons to faint away, and even for a time lose the power of their senses. A less sight than this, even the sight of Solomon's glory, made Sheba's queen astonished; and a still lesser sight than that, even a sight of Joseph's waggons, made holy Jacob to faint, and for a while, as it were, die away. Daniel, when admitted to a distant view of this excellent glory, fell down at the feet of the angel as one dead. And if a distant view of this glory be so excellent, what must the actual possession of it be? If the first fruits are so glorious, how infinitely must the harvest exceed in glory?

And now, what shall I, or, indeed, what can I well say more to excite you, even you that are yet strangers to Christ, to come and walk with God? If you love honour, pleasure, and a crown of glory, come, seek it where alone it can be found. Come, put ye on the Lord Jesus. Come, haste ye away and walk with God, and make no longer provision for the flesh, to fulfil the lust thereof. Stop, stop, O sinner! turn ye, turn ye, O ye unconverted men, for the end of that way you are now walking in, however right it may seem in your blinded eyes, will be death, even eternal destruction both of body and soul. Make no longer tarrying, I say: at your peril I charge you, step not one step further on in your present walk. For how knowest thou, O man, but the next step thou takest may be into hell? Death may seize thee, judgment find thee, and then the great gulf will be fixed between thee and endless glory for ever and ever. O think of these things, all ye that are unwilling to walk with God. Lay them to heart. Shew yourselves men, and in the strength of Jesus say, Farewell, lust of the flesh, I will no more walk with thee! farewell, lust of the eye, and pride of life! Farewell, carnal acquaintance and enemies of the cross, I will no more walk and be intimate with you! Welcome Jesus, welcome thy word, welcome thy ordinances, welcome thy Spirit, welcome thy people, I will henceforth walk with you. O that there may be in you such a mind! God will set his almighty fiat to it, and seal it with the broad seal of heaven, even the signet of his holy Spirit. Yes, he will, though you have been walking with, and following after, the devices and desires of your desperately wicked hearts ever since you have been born. 'I, the high and lofty One', says the great Jehovah, 'that inhabiteth eternity, will dwell with the humble and contrite heart, even with the man that trembleth at my word.' The blood, even the precious blood of Jesus Christ, if you come to the Father in and through him, shall cleanse you from all sin.

But the text leads me to speak to you that are saints as well as to you that are open and unconverted sinners. I need not tell you, that walking with God is not only honourable, but pleasant and profitable also; for ye know it by happy experience, and will find it more and more so every day. Only give me leave to stir up your pure minds by way of remembrance, and to beseech you by the mercies of God in Christ Jesus, to take heed to yourselves, and walk closer with your God than you have in days past: for the nearer you walk with God, the more you will enjoy of him whose presence is life, and be the better prepared for being placed at his right hand, where are pleasures for evermore. O do not follow Jesus afar off! O be not so formal, so dead and stupid in your attendance on holy ordinances! Do not so shamefully forsake the assembling yourselves together, or be so niggardly or indifferent about the things of God. Remember what Jesus says of the church of Laodicea, 'Because thou art neither hot nor cold, I will spew thee out of my

[181]

mouth'. Think of the love of Jesus, and let that love constrain you to keep near unto him; and though you die for him, do not deny him, do not keep at a distance from him in any wise.

One word to my brethren in the ministry that are here present, and I have done. You see, my brethren, my heart is full; I could almost say it is too big to speak, and yet too big to be silent, without dropping a word to you. For does not the text speak in a particular manner to those who have the honour of being styled the ambassadors of Christ, and stewards of the mysteries of God. I observed at the beginning of this discourse, that Enoch in all probability was a public person, and a flaming preacher. Though he be dead, does he not yet speak to us, to quicken our zeal, and make us more active in the service of our glorious and everblessed Master? How did Enoch preach! How did Enoch walk with God, though he lived in a wicked and adulterous generation! Let us then follow him, as he followed Jesus Christ, and ere long, where he is there shall we be also. He is now entered into his rest: yet a little while and we shall enter into ours, and that too much sooner than he did. He sojourned here below three hundred years; but blessed be God, the days of man are now shortened, and in a few days our walk will be over. The Judge is before the door: he that cometh will come, and will not tarry: his reward is with him. And we shall all (if we are zealous for the Lord of hosts) ere long shine as the stars in the firmament, in the kingdom of our heavenly Father, for ever and ever. To Him, the blessed Jesus, and eternal Spirit, be all honour and glory, now, and to all eternity. *Amen*, and *Amen*.

THE GOOD SHEPHERD
[A FAREWELL SERMON][1]

My sheep hear my voice, and I know them, and they
follow me. And I give unto them eternal life, and they
shall never perish, neither shall any pluck them out
of my hand. *John* 10.27, 28

It is a common, and I believe, generally speaking, my dear
hearers, a true saying, that bad manners beget good laws.
Whether this will hold good in every particular, in respect
to the affairs of this world, I am persuaded the observation
is very pertinent in respect to the things of another: I mean
bad manners, bad treatment, bad words, have been over-
ruled by the sovereign grace of God, to produce, and to be
the cause of, the best sermons that were ever delivered from
the mouth of the God-man, Christ Jesus.

One would have imagined, that as he came clothed with
divine efficience, as he came with divine credentials, as he
spake as never man spake, no one should have been able to
have resisted the wisdom with which he spake; one would
imagine, they should have been so struck with the demonstration of the Spirit, that with one consent they should all
own that he was 'that prophet that was to be raised up like
unto Moses'. But you seldom find our Lord preaching a
sermon, but something or other that he said was cavilled
at; nay, their enmity frequently broke through all good
manners. They often, therefore, interrupted him whilst he

[1] The last sermon which Whitefield preached in London, on Wednesday, August 30th, 1769, before his final departure to America.

was preaching, which shews the enmity of their hearts long before God permitted it to be in their power to shed his innocent blood. If we look no further than this chapter, where he presents himself as a good shepherd, one that laid down his life for his sheep; we see the best return he had, was to be looked upon as possessed or distracted; for we are told, that there was a division therefore again among the Jews for these sayings, and many of them said, 'He hath a devil, and is mad; why hear ye him?' If the master of the house was served so, pray what are the servants to expect? Others, a little more sober-minded, said, 'These are not the words of him that hath a devil'; the devil never used to preach or act in this way; 'Can a devil open the eyes of the blind?' So he had some friends among these rabble. This did not discourage our Lord; he goes on in his work; and we shall never, never go on with the work of God, till, like our Master, we are willing to go through good and through evil report; and let the devil see we are not so complaisant as to stop one moment for his barking at us as we go along.

We are told, that our Lord was at Jerusalem at the feast of the dedication, and it was winter; the feast of dedication held, I think, seven or eight days, for the commemoration of the restoration of the temple and altar, after its profanation by Antiochus. Now this was certainly a mere human institution, and had no divine image, had no divine superscription upon it; and yet I do not find that our blessed Lord and Master preached against it; I do not find that he spent his time about this; his heart was too big with superior things; and I believe when we, like him, are filled with the Holy Ghost, we shall not entertain our audiences with disputes about rites and ceremonies, but shall treat upon the essentials of the gospel, and then rites and ceremonies will appear with more indifference. Our Lord does not say, that he would not go up to the feast, for, on the contrary, he did go there, not so much as to keep the feast, as to have an opportunity to spread the gospel-net; and that should be our method, not to follow disputing; and it is the glory of the Methodists, that we have been now forty years, and, I thank God, there has not been one single pamphlet written by any of our preachers, about the non-essentials of religion.

Our Lord always made the best of every opportunity; and we are told, 'he walked in the temple in Solomon's porch'. One would have thought the scribes and Pharisees would have put him in one of their stalls, and have complimented him with desiring him to preach: no, they let him walk in Solomon's porch. Some think he walked by himself, no body choosing to keep company with him. Methinks I see him walking and looking at the temple, and foreseeing within himself how soon it would be destroyed; he walked pensive, to see the dreadful calamities that would come upon the land, for not knowing the day of its visitation; and it was to let the world see he was not afraid to appear in public: he walked, as much as to say, Have any of you any thing to say to me? and he put himself in their way, that if they had any things to ask him, he was ready to resolve them; and to shew them, that though they had treated him so ill, yet he was ready to preach salvation to them.

In the 24th verse we are told, 'Then came the Jews round about him, and said unto him, How long dost thou make us doubt?' They came round about him when they saw him walking in Solomon's porch; now, say they, we will have him, now we will attack him. And now was fulfilled that passage in the Psalms, 'they compassed me about like bees', to sting me, or rather like wasps. Now, say they, we will get him in the middle of us, and see what sort of a man he is; we will see whether we cannot conquer him; they came to him, and they say, 'How long dost thou make us to doubt?' Now this seems a plausible question, 'How long dost thou make us to doubt?' Pray how long, sir, do you intend to keep us in suspense? Some think the words will bear this interpretation; Pray, sir, how long do you intend thus to steal away our hearts? they would represent him to be a designing man, like Absalom, to get the people on his side, and then set up himself for the Messiah; thus carnal minds always interpret good men's actions. But the meaning seems to be this, they were doubting concerning Christ; doubting Christians may think it is God's fault that they doubt, but, God knows, it is all their own. 'How long dost thou make us to doubt?' I wish you would speak a little plainer, sir, and not let us have any more of your parables. Pray let us know who you are, let us have it from your own mouth; 'if thou be the Christ, tell us plainly'; and I do not doubt, but they put on a very sanctified face, and looked very demure; 'if thou be the Christ, tell us plainly', intending to catch him: if he do not say he is the Christ, we will say he is ashamed of his own cause; if he tells us plainly that he is the Christ, then we will impeach him to the governor, we will go and tell the governor that this man says he is the Messiah; now we know of no Messiah, but what is to jostle Cæsar out of his throne. — The devil always wants to make it believed that God's people, who are the most loyal people in the world, are rebels to the government under which they live; 'If thou be the Christ, tell us plainly'. Our Lord does not let them wait long for an answer; honesty can soon speak: 'I told you, and ye believed not; the works that I do in my Father's name, they bear witness of me'. Had our Lord said, I am the Messiah, they would have taken him up; he knew that, and therefore he joined 'the wisdom of the serpent' with 'the innocence of the dove'; says he, I appeal to my works and doctrine, and if you will not infer from them that I am the Messiah, I have no further argument. 'But', he adds, 'ye believe not, because ye are not of my sheep.' He complains twice; for their unbelief was the greatest grief of heart to Christ: then he goes on in the words of our text, 'My sheep hear my voice, and I know them, and they follow me. And I give unto them eternal life, and they shall never perish, neither shall any pluck them out of my hand'. My sheep hear my voice; you think to puzzle me, you thing to chagrin me with this kind of conduct, but you are mistaken; you do not believe on me, because you are not of my sheep. The great Mr Stoddard of New England, (and no place under heaven produces greater divines than New England), preached once from these words, 'But ye believe not, because ye are not of my sheep'; a very strange text to preach upon, to convince a congregation! yet God so blessed it, that two or three hundred souls were awakened by that sermon: God grant such success to attend the labours of all his faithful ministers.

'My sheep hear my voice, and they follow me.' It is very remarkable, there are but two sorts of people mentioned in scripture: it does not say that the Baptists and Independents, nor the Methodists and Presbyterians; no, Jesus Christ divides the whole world into but two classes, sheep and goats: the Lord give us to see this morning to which of these classes we belong.

But it is observable, believers are always compared to something that is good and profitable, and unbelievers are always described by something that is bad, and good for little or nothing.

If you ask me why Christ's people are called sheep, as God shall enable me, I will give you a short, and I hope it will be to you an answer of peace. Sheep, you know, generally love to be together; we say a flock of sheep, we do not say a herd of sheep; sheep are little creatures, and Christ's people may be called sheep, because they are little in the eyes of the world, and they are yet less in their own eyes. O, some people think, if the great men were on our side, if we had king, lords, and commons on our side, I mean if they were all true believers, O if we had all the kings upon the earth on our side! Suppose you had: alas! alas! do you think the church would go on the better? Why, if it were fashionable to be a Methodist at court, if it were fashionable to be a Methodist abroad, they would go with a Bible or a hymn-book, instead of a novel; but religion never thrives under too much sun-shine. 'Not many mighty, not many noble, are called, but God hath chosen the foolish things of the world to confound the wise, and God hath chosen the weak things of the world to confound the things which are mighty.' Dr Watts says, Here and there I see a king, and here and there a great man, in heaven, but their number is but small.

Sheep are looked upon to be the most harmless, quiet creatures that God hath made: O may God, of his infinite mercy, give us to know that we are his sheep, by our having this blessed temper infused into our hearts by the Holy Ghost. 'Learn of me', saith our blessed Lord; what to do? to work miracles? no; 'Learn of me, for I am meek and lowly in heart'. A very good man, now living, said once, if there be any particular temper I desire more than another, it is the grace of *meekness*, quietly to bear bad treatment, to forget and to forgive: and at the same time that I am sensible I am injured, not to be overcome of evil, but to have grace given me to overcome evil with good. To the honour of Moses, it is declared, that he was the meekest man upon earth. Meekness is necessary for people in power; a man that is passionate is dangerous. Every governor should have a warm temper, but a man of an unrelenting, unforgiving temper, is no more fit for government than Phaethon to drive the chariot of the sun; he only sets the world on fire.

You all know, that sheep of all creatures in the world are the most apt to stray and be lost; Christ's people may justly, in that respect, be compared to sheep; therefore, in the introduction to our morning service, we say, 'We have erred and strayed from thy ways like lost sheep'. Turn out a horse, or a dog, and they will find their way home, but a sheep wanders about; he bleats here and there, as much as to say, Dear stranger, shew me my way home again; thus Christ's sheep are too apt to wander from the fold; having their eye off the great Shepherd, they go into this field and that field, over this hedge and that, and often return home with the loss of their wool.

But at the same time sheep are the most useful creatures in the world; they manure the land, and thereby prepare it for the seed; they clothe our bodies with wool, and there is not the least part of a sheep but is useful to man: O my brethren, God grant that you and I may, in this respect, answer the character of sheep. The world says, because we preach faith we deny good works; this is the usual objection against the doctrine of imputed righteousness, but it is a slander, an impudent slander. It was a maxim in the first reformers' time, that though the *Arminians* preached up

[189]

good works, you must go to the *Calvinists* for them. Christ's sheep study to be useful, and to clothe all they can; we should labour with our hands, that we may have to give to all those that need.

Believers consider Christ's property in them; he says, 'my sheep': O blessed be God for that little, dear, great word *My*. We are his eternal election: "the sheep which thou hast given me', says Christ. They were given by God the Father to Christ Jesus, in the covenant made between the Father and the Son from all eternity. They that are not led to see this, I wish them better heads; though, I believe, numbers that are against it have got better hearts: the Lord help us to bear with one another where there is an honest heart.

He calls them 'My sheep'; they are his by purchase. O sinner, sinner, you are come this morning to hear a poor creature take 'his last farewell': but I want you to forget the creature that is preaching, I want to lead you further than the Tabernacle: Where do you want to lead us? why, to mount Calvary, there to see at what an expense of blood Christ purchased those whom he calls his own; he redeemed them with his own blood, so that they are not only his by eternal election, but also by actual redemption in time; and they were given to him by the Father, upon condition that he should redeem them by his heart's blood. It was a hard bargain, but Christ was willing to strike the bargain, that you and I might not be damned for ever.

They are his, because they are enabled in a day of God's power voluntarily to give themselves up unto him; Christ says of these sheep, especially, 'that they hear his voice, and that they follow him'. Will you be so good as to mind that! Here is an allusion to a shepherd; now in some places in scripture, the shepherd is represented as going after his sheep; 2 Sam 7.8, Ps 78.71. That is our way in England; but in the Eastern nations, the shepherds generally went before; they held up their crook, and they had a particular call that the sheep understood. Now, says Christ, 'My sheep hear my voice'. 'This is my beloved Son', saith God, 'hear ye him.' And again, 'The dead shall hear the voice of the Son of God, and live': now the question is, what do we understand by hearing Christ's voice?

First, we hear Moses' voice, we hear the voice of the law; there is no going to Mount Zion but by the way of mount Sinai; that is the right straight road. I know some say, they do not know when they were converted; those are, I believe, very few: generally, nay, I may say almost always, God deals otherwise. Some are, indeed, called sooner by the Lord than others, but before they are made to see the glory of God, they must hear the voice of the law; so you must hear the voice of the law before ever you will be savingly called unto God. You never throw off your cloak in a storm, but you hug it the closer; so the law makes a man hug close his corruptions, (Rom 7.7, 8, 9) but when the gospel of the Son of God shines into their souls, then they throw off the corruptions which they have hugged so closely; they hear his voice saying, Son, daughter, be of good cheer, thy sins, which are many, are all forgiven thee. 'They hear his voice'; that bespeaks the habitual temper of their minds: the wicked hear the voice of the devil, the lusts of the flesh, the lusts of the eye, and the pride of life; and Christ's sheep themselves attended to it before conversion; but when called afterwards by God, they hear the voice of a Redeemer's blood speaking peace unto them, they hear the voice of his word and of his Spirit.

The consequence of hearing his voice, and the proof that

[191]

we do hear his voice, will be — to follow him. Jesus said unto his disciples, 'If any man will come after me, let him deny himself, and take up his cross and follow me'. And it is said of the saints in glory, that 'they followed the Lamb whithersoever he went'. Wherever the shepherd turns his crook, and the sheep hear his voice, they follow him; they often tread upon one another, and hurt one another, they are in such haste in their way to heaven. Following Christ means following him through life, following him in every word and gesture, following him out of one clime into another. 'Bid me come to thee upon the water', said Peter: and if we are commanded to go over the water for Christ, God, of his infinite mercy, follow us! We must first be sure that the great Shepherd points his crook for us: but this is the character of a true servant of Christ, that he endeavours to follow Christ in thought, word, and work.

Now, my brethren, before we go further, as this is the last opportunity I shall have of speaking to you for some months, if we live; some of you, I suppose, do not choose, in general, to rise so soon as you have this morning; now I hope the world did not get into your hearts before you left your beds; now you are here, do let me entreat you to inquire whether you belong to Christ's sheep, or no. Man, woman, sinner, put thy hand to thy heart, and answer me. Didst thou ever hear Christ's voice so as to follow him, to give up thyself without reserve to him? I verily do believe from my inmost soul, (and that is my comfort, now I am about to take my leave of you,) that I am preaching to a vast body, a multitude of dear, precious souls, who, if it were proper for you to speak, would say, Thanks be unto God, that we can follow Jesus in the character of sheep, though we are ashamed to think how often we wander from him, and what little fruit we bring unto him; if that is the language of your hearts, I wish you joy; welcome, welcome, dear soul, to Christ. O blessed be God for his rich grace, his distinguishing, sovereign, electing love, by which he has distinguished you and me. And if he has been pleased to let you hear his voice, through the ministration of a poor miserable sinner, a poor, but happy pilgrim, may the Lord Jesus Christ have all the glory.

If you belong to Jesus Christ, he is speaking of you; for, says he, 'I know my sheep'. 'I know them'; what does that mean? Why, he knows their number, he knows their names, he knows every one for whom he died; and if there were to be one missing for whom Christ died, God the Father would send him down again from heaven to fetch him. 'Of all', saith he, 'that thou hast given me, have I lost none.' Christ knows his sheep; he not only knows their number, but the words speak the peculiar knowledge and notice he takes of them; he takes as much care of each of them, as if there were but that one single sheep in the world. To the hypocrite he saith, 'Verily, I know you not'; but he knows his saints, he is acquainted with all their sorrows, their trials, and temptations. He bottles up all their tears, he knows their domestic trials, he knows their inward corruptions, he knows all their wanderings, and he takes care to fetch them back again. I remember, I heard good Dr Marryat, who was a good market-language preacher, once say at Pinner's-hall, (I hope that pulpit will be always filled with such preachers), 'God has got a great dog to fetch his sheep back', says he. Do not you know, that when the sheep wander, the shepherd sends his dog after them, to fetch them back again? So when Christ's sheep wander, he lets the devil go after them, and suffers him to bark at them, who, instead of driving them farther off, is made a means to bring them back again to Christ's fold.

There is a precious word I would have you take notice of, 'I know them', that may comfort you under all your trials. We sometimes think that Christ does not hear our prayers, that he does not know us; we are ready to suspect that he has forgotten to be gracious; but what a mercy it is that he does know us. We accuse one another, we turn devils to one another, are accusers of the brethren; and what will support two of God's people when judged by one another but this, Lord, thou knowest my integrity, thou knowest how matters are with me?

But, my brethren, here is something better, here is good news for you; what is that? say you: why, 'I give unto them eternal life, and they shall never perish, neither shall any pluck them out of my hand'. O that the words may come to your hearts with as much warmth and power as they did to mine thirty-five years ago. I never prayed against any corruption I had in my life, so much as I did against going into holy orders so soon as my friends were for having me go: and bishop Benson was pleased to honour me with peculiar friendship, so as to offer me preferment, or do any thing for me. My friends wanted me to mount the church betimes, they wanted me to knock my head against the pulpit too young; but how some young men stand up here and there and preach, I do not know how it may be to them; but God knows how deep a concern entering into the ministry and preaching, was to me; I have prayed a thousand times, till the sweat has dropped from my face like rain, that God, of his infinite mercy, would not let me enter the church before he called me to, and thrust me forth in, his work. I remember once in Gloucester (I know the room,

I look up at the window when I am there and walk along the street; I know the window, the bedside, and the floor, upon which I have lain prostrate) I said, Lord, I cannot go, I shall be puffed up with pride, and fall into the condemnation of the devil; Lord, do not let me go yet; I pleaded to be at Oxford two or three years more; I intended to make an hundred and fifty sermons, and thought I would set up with a good stock in trade but I remember praying, wrestling, and striving with God; I said, I am undone, I am unfit to preach in thy great name, send me not, pray, Lord, send me not yet. I wrote to all my friends in town and country, to pray against the bishop's solicitations, but they insisted I should go into orders before I was twenty-two. After all their solicitations, these words came into my mind, 'My Sheep hear my voice, and none shall pluck them out of my hand'. O may the words be blessed to you, my dear friends, that I am parting with, as they were to me when they came warm upon my heart; then, and not till then, I said, Lord, I will go, send me when thou wilt. I remember when I was in a place called Dover-Island, near Georgia, we put in with bad winds; I had an hundred and fifty in family to maintain, and not a single farthing to do it with, in the dearest part of the king's dominions; I remember, I told a minister of Christ, now in heaven, 'I had these words once, sir, "Nothing shall pluck you out of my hand". O, says he, take comfort from them, you may be sure God will be as good as his word, if he never tells you so again.' And our Lord knew his poor sheep would be always doubting they should never reach heaven, therefore says he, 'I give to them eternal life, and they shall never perish'.

Here are in our text three blessed declarations, or promises:

First. *I know them.*

Second. *They shall never perish;* though they often think they shall perish by the hand of their lusts and corruptions; they think they shall perish by the deceitfulness of their hearts; but Christ says, 'They shall never perish'. I have brought them out of the world to myself, and do you think I will let them go to hell after that? 'I give to them eternal life'; pray mind that; not, I will, but I do. Some talk of being justified at the day of judgment; that is nonsense; if we are not justified here, we shall not be justified there. He gives them eternal life, that is, the earnest, the pledge, and assurance of it. The indwelling of the Spirit of God here, is the earnest of glory hereafter.

Third. *Neither shall any pluck them out of my hand.* He holds them in his hand, that is, he holds them by his power; none shall pluck them thence. There is always something plucking at Christ's sheep; the devil, the lust of the flesh, the lust of the eye, and the pride of life, all try to pluck them out of Christ's hand. O my brethren, they need not pluck us, yet we help all three to pluck ourselves out of the hand of Jesus; but 'none shall pluck them out of my hand', says Christ. 'I give to them eternal life. I am going to heaven to prepare a place for them, and there they shall be.' O my brethren, if it were not for keeping you too long, and too much exhausting my own spirits, I could call upon you to leap for joy; there is not a more blessed text to support the final perseverance of the saints; and I am astonished any poor souls, and good people I hope too, can fight against the doctrine of the perseverance of the saints : What if a person say they should persevere in wickedness? Ah! that is an abuse of the doctrine; what, because some people spoil good food, are we never to eat it? But, my brethren, upon this text I can leave my cares, and all my friends, and all Christ's sheep, to the protection of Christ Jesus' never-failing love.

I thought this morning, when I came here, riding from the other end of the town, it was to me like coming to be executed publicly; and when the carriage turned just at the end of the walk, and I saw you running here, O, thinks I, it is like a person now coming just to the place where he is to be executed. When I went up to put on my gown, I thought it was just like dressing myself to be made a public spectacle to shed my blood for Christ. I take all heaven and earth to witness, and God and the holy angels to witness, that though I had preferment enough offered me, that though the bishop took me in his arms, and offered me two parishes before I was two-and-twenty, and always took me to his table; though I had preferment enough offered me when I was ordained, thou, O God, knowest, that when the bishop put his hand upon my head, I looked for no other preferment than publicly to suffer for the Lamb of God: in this spirit I came out, in this spirit I came up to this metropolis. I was thinking, when I read of Jacob's going over the brook with a staff, that I could not say I had so much as a staff, but I came up without a friend, I went to Oxford without a friend, I had not a servant, I had not a single person to introduce me; but God, by his Holy Spirit, was pleased to raise me up to preach for his great name's sake: through his divine Spirit I continue to this day, and feel my affections are as strong as ever towards the work and the people of the living God. The congregations at both ends of the town are dear to me: God has honoured me to build this and the other place; and, blessed be his name, when he called me to Georgia at first, and I left all London affairs to God's care, when I had most of the churches in London open to me, and had twelve or fourteen constables to keep the doors, that people might not crowd too much; I had offers of hundreds then to settle in London, yet I gave it all up to turn pilgrim for God, to go into a foreign clime; and I hope with that same single intention I am going now . . .

Now, I must come to the hardest part I have to act; I was afraid when I came out from home, that I could not bear the shock, but I hope the Lord Jesus Christ will help me to bear it, and help you to give me up to the blessed God, let him do with me what he will. This is the thirteenth time of my crossing the mighty waters; it is a little difficult at this time of life; and though my spirits are improved in some degree, yet weakness is the best of my strength: but I am clear as light in my call and God fills me with a peace that is unutterable, which a stranger intermeddles not with: into his hands I commend my spirit; and I beg that this may be the language of your hearts: Lord, keep him, let nothing pluck him out of thy hands. I expect many a trial while I am on board, Satan always meets me there; but that God who has kept me, I believe will keep me. I thank God, I have the honour of leaving every thing quite well and easy at both ends of the town; and, my dear hearers, my prayers to God shall be, that nothing may pluck you out of Christ's hands. Witness against me, if I ever set up a party for myself. Did ever any minister, or could any minister in the world say, that I ever spoke against any one going to any dear minister? I thank God, that he has enabled me to be always strengthening the hands of all, though some have afterwards been ashamed to own me. I declare to you, that I believe God will be with me, and will strengthen me; and I believe it is in answer to your prayers that God is pleased to revive my spirits: may the Lord help you to pray on. If

I am drowned in the waves, I will say, while I am drowning, Lord, take care of my London, take care of my English friends, let nothing pluck them out of thy hands.

And as Christ has given us eternal life, O my brethren, some of you, I doubt not, will be gone to him before my return; but, my dear brethren, my dear hearers, never mind that; we shall part, but it will be to meet again for ever. I dare not meet you now, I cannot bear your coming to me, to part from me; it cuts me to the heart, and quite overcomes me, but by and by all parting will be over, and all tears shall be wiped away from our eyes. God grant that none that weep now at my parting, may weep at our meeting at the day of judgment; and if you never were among Christ's sheep before, may Christ Jesus bring you now. O come, come, see what it is to have eternal life; do not refuse it; haste, sinner, haste away: may the great, the good Shepherd, draw your souls. Oh! if you never heard his voice before, God grant you may hear it now; that I may have this comfort when I am gone, that I had the last time of my leaving you, that some souls are awakened at the parting sermon. O that it may be a farewell sermon to you; that it may be a means of your taking a farewell of the world, the lust of the flesh, the lust of the eye, and the pride of life. O come! come! come! to the Lord Jesus Christ; to him I leave you.

And you, dear sheep, that are already in his hands, O may God keep you from wandering; God keep you near Christ's feet; I do not care what shepherds keep you, so as you are kept near the great Shepherd and Bishop of souls. The Lord God keep you, lift up the light of his countenance upon you, and give you peace. *Amen.*